THE
LATIN
CENTURY

The Increasing Impact of Latinos in the 21st Century

Federico Maese, MD

Table of Contents

To the millions of past, present and future Latinos, who were, are, and will continue to be an integral people who have made and will continue to make significant contributions to this amazing country.

INTRODUCTION

We the people of the United States of America, in this 21st century, find ourselves living and experiencing a rapidly changing society, far more diverse than at any other time in the history of the country. Some would opine this is an expected phenomenon. My grandfather, Federico Sanchez, prior to his passing in 2001 at age eighty-eight, shared with me that Latinos would in time become a powerful force in the U.S. He had a particular bias in this regard. He had not been pleased that I made the choice to stay in the U.S. after completing my medical training, as opposed to returning to Mexico. He harbored, as many Mexican historians still do, painful memories of the Guadalupe Hidalgo Treaty of 1848 that resulted in Mexico ceding some fifty-five percent of its territory to the U.S. My grandfather felt that it had been an unjust war largely driven by Manifest Destiny, the Monroe Doctrine, and pure greed. He often said Mexicans would gradually take those territories back, but not by waging war. He alleged Mexicans, through their family values, faith, work ethic, and tendency to have large families, would inevitably, albeit gradually, become an integral and necessary part of most aspects of U.S. society. He was correct.

Aside from the dramatic growth of the Latino population in the U.S., now about twenty percent of the entire population, the estimated 2020 Latino contribution was an extraordinary $2.8 trillion in GDP, up from $2.1 trillion in 2015 and $1.7 trillion in 2010. If in 2020, Latinos in the U.S. were an independent country, they would have the fifth largest GDP in the world, outpacing the United Kingdom, France, Italy, Canada, India, Brazil, and Mexico. Currently only Germany, Japan, China, and the U.S. are higher. Furthermore, it is estimated by 2050 one in four individuals living in the U.S. will be of Latino descent. At this rate of growth, some prognosticate over the coming decades, Latinos as a bloc will continue to add GDP to the U.S. economy at a rate far higher than non-Latino populations.

The performance of Latinos during the 2020 Coronavirus pandemic is important to note here. Despite the challenges of the pandemic, with government-mandated lockdowns, Latino real wage salary and income *increased* by 6.7% while the non-Latino income *decreased* by 1.1%. From the early phases of the pandemic and through every re-imposition of business and social lockdowns, Latino extraordinary work ethic overcame each subsequent wave of Covid-19 disease transmission, returning to work or seeking work with urgency, such that Latino labor force participation grew to 6.5% points higher than for non-Latinos. Although in 2020 the U.S. Latino GDP contracted by 0.8%, compared to 4.4% for non-Latinos, and European nations like France and the U.K. decreased by 8.2% and 9.8% respectively, it was this contribution that helped the U.S. maintain its economy without significant shrinkage. But it came at a tremendous hardship to distinct groups of Latinos.

Despite pre-pandemic Latinos' great health outcomes, they as a group had among the highest rates of hospitalization and deaths in the U.S. related to Covid-19, which became the number one cause of death among Latinos. This can in part be explained by Latinos' work ethic and unique family dynamics, and on the higher prevalence of obesity and diabetes. However, less access to healthcare education, infrastructure, and resources also surely played a key role. These economic numbers reflect the significant sacrifices made by Latinos during the pandemic, enormously benefiting the broader U.S. economy. Sadly, such facts have been ignored by main-stream media outlets. As have been the great sacrifices many Latinos made to keep working when most of the world shut down.

Beyond my grandfather's prediction of the twenty-first century's gradual browning of America and the growing economic contributions by Latinos to the U.S. economy, there are many other aspects of society impacted by this group of peoples. Latinos are an extremely diverse group, each dependent on their nation of origin, with their own history, linguistic idiosyncrasies, and cultural and political influences. Although Latinos may share language, genetics, religious backgrounds, and conservative values, the diversity within and between each group is abundant, often shaped by multiple factors such as country of origin, family history, educational level, profession, religion, ingrained cultural beliefs, and the local and national political landscape. This rich diversity is highlighted by clear differences between the three largest Latino groups: New York Puerto Ricans, Florida Cubans, and Mexicans predominantly in the southwest.

The recent waves of immigrants this century, and the more than five million who have crossed into the U.S. over the last two years, most of these unvetted, are rapidly changing the Latino and overall population landscape in the U.S. Presently, most of these new migrants are not from Mexico as in prior decades, when the economy was stronger, but instead from Central American triangle countries and South American and Caribbean nations that continue to experience social instability due to widespread corruption, poverty, drug-related crime, and political unrest. It is important to recognize that economic or family-sponsored migrants are different than those arriving in the U.S. as refugees. The former group voluntarily depart their nation of origin whereas the latter, to avoid life-threatening persecution, are forced to leave their home country. This difference is of critical importance to the U.S. economy and society. Rates of assimilation, adaptation, and acceptance of the Anglo-American society may not be accomplished at similar levels by these groups, especially within one or two generations. Refugees are more likely to maintain the cultural, religious, and linguistic hegemony of their home country, especially as they come to settle in close-knit communities with others from their native land. The individual and family emotional upheaval of many immigrants to the U.S. should not be underestimated. Integration to U.S. society at large often presents challenges to some immigrants, especially those from a vastly different culture, with lesser education, and non-English speakers. Poor assimilation and adaptation to U.S. society, more so for single individuals, frequently results in fewer employment opportunities, cultural isolation, and mental health issues such as depression. Even if these individuals manage to carve out an adequate living, often sending funds back to support family in their country of origin, many remain isolated and unintegrated to the greater U.S. society for the long term. This phenomenon of people seeking a better life for their families and undertaking a risky voluntary migration is far from new, nor is it unexpected. Historically, an economically and militarily successful empire or country will attract migrants seeking opportunity and a better life, especially from poorer regions or nations. This has been the history of the world and will continue to be the case.

In addition to migrants able to make it to the U.S. through relative geographical closeness, many new migrants to the U.S. are also arriving from more distant destinations including the Caribbean, Middle East, and Southeast Asia. These are all part of the net international migration (NIM) that promises to rapidly grow the U.S. population in the next thirty years. According to the Pew Research Center the U.S. population in 2050 will reach between 422 and 458 million, depending on low versus high NIM. By the same year, the Latino population will be 132 million and as high as 143 million, or about 29% to 31% of the U.S. population, again depending on NIM. By comparison, in 2050 the Pew Research Center projects the population of non-Hispanic whites will be 45%, blacks 13% and Asians 8%. This largest Latino minority will in time, before the end of the twenty-first century, will become the majority. I say this because Latinos are a young, child-bearing population. Latinos, especially those of Mexican descent, have about the highest fertility rates in the U.S. and possess traditional family-oriented, conservative values built on a bedrock of putting family first, a strong work ethic, and active faith. Given the phenomenon known as the "Hispanic Paradox," or observation that Latinos have the highest longevity in the U.S., except for Asians, despite less access to healthcare resources and higher incidence than whites and blacks of diabetes, it is likely more Latinos will grow old surrounded by their grandchildren and great grandchildren.

Aside from the dramatic growth of the Latino population in the U.S. in the twenty-first century, and the growing GDP contribution to the economy, Latinos have rapidly become even more important to the present and future overall wellbeing of the U.S. This implies a national and international stage. Without Latinos, the U.S. will not maintain its current precarious status as the leader of the "free world," nor experience growth and prosperity. Effective Latino participation across multiple areas of U.S. society, beyond manual labor, is and will be increasingly essential. The recent growing Latino vote, especially since 2016, political involvement, including new candidates running for public office, higher graduation rates from two- and four-year colleges and universities over the last decade, are all clear signs Latinos have become aware of the importance of these achievements, and are more invested than at any other time in the present U.S. society and their future within it.

As Latino labor force participation continues to grow, including entrepreneurial endeavors and investment in financial markets, unfortunately, in other areas Latino influence and priorities remain lacking. For example, the delivery of healthcare resources and services in the era of the Affordable Care Act is not meeting the needs of the at large different Latino communities. A better healthcare model is urgently needed, especially one that can institute education on health and nutrition, preventive strategies, and effective control of chronic diseases. Another example is the fact that immigration policies remain insufficient, especially with the current open southern border crisis. It is estimated that some twenty to thirty million undocumented Latinos are currently living in the U.S., many who have been contributing to the U.S. economy for years. This issue and DACA (dreamers), both need a resolution to this "in limbo" situation. It has become evident that Latino communities across the southwest border states, among others, have become politically active with the intent of protecting their families from the criminality brought into their backyards by the millions pouring over the border illegally. Drug and human trafficking, violence, and the fact most of these communities do not have the resources to absorb thousands of undocumented migrants, has only recently exploded into the national dialogue. The resolution cannot continue to be the porous open border and subsequent transportation of these unfortunate people to northern states. The criminality extends to many deciding to risk the perilous journey from their home country, with thousands victimized and even killed along the way. Latinos, as well as most citizens in the U.S., are demanding an immediate solution.

The same can be said for the recent waves of crime, on the increase since 2020, affecting mostly large urban centers in the U.S. Latinos and Backs have been adversely affected by recent defund the police type policies, progressive district attorneys, no-bail statutes, and by letting criminals out early, many who should remain incarcerated. Latinos at large have had little say in the experimental institution of most of these policies. The mainstream media tendency to downplay such criminality has been catastrophic for minorities.

Other areas where Latinos continue to be neglected, marginalized, and their opinion not considered important or even relevant, despite their growing economic prowess, are the relationships with mainstream media, big-tech companies, the entertainment businesses, including Hollywood, and even some professional sports.

Despite these troublesome relationships that demand immediate amelioration, the positive aspect that keeps Latinos well-grounded, and emotionally content, is the family. Nuclear and extended family bonds remain a deep-rooted cultural priority for most Latinos, with the all-too-common scenario of several generations coinhabiting in a single household. This generational togetherness, an innate Latino attribute, fosters respect, dignity, and identity. For most Latinos, mother and father are the role models and heroes of their journey in life. No matter what adversity is to be confronted, what difficulties life may bring, Latinos have this most precious and rich resource at their side: family. With all this in mind, the following chapters will delve into important aspects of present U.S. society and the reasons why these one hundred years, the twenty-first century, will come to be known as "The Latin Century."

WHO ARE THE LATINOS?

Pew Research Center calculated, based on the 2021 American Community Surveys (U.S. Census Bureau), the Latino origin of the 62.53 million legal Latinos living in the U.S. This was based on self-described ancestry, lineage, heritage, nationality group, or country of birth. Some 59.5% were Mexican, 9.3% Puerto Rican, 4.0% Salvadorean, 3.8% Cuban, 3.8% Dominican, 2.8% Guatemalan, 2.2% Columbian, 1.8% Honduran, 1.3% Ecuadorian, 1.2% Peruvian, 1.1% Venezuelan, and all other groups less than 1% (see table). In the period from 2010 to 2021, Latinos in the U.S. grew by 23%, that is from 16% to 19.4% of the total U.S. population. In contrast, non-Latino Whites decreased from 64.7% to 60% and Blacks remained at about 13%. This growth is expected to continue such that by 2030, Latinos will be 23% of the U.S. population, by 2050 about 30%, and by the end of the twenty-first century Latinos will be at least 40%. By then the non-Latino White population will 35% to 40%!

It is estimated those of Mexican descent will continue to be greater than 50% of the Latino population. The above statistics do not take into consideration the estimated significant numbers of undocumented immigrants noted previously, the majority originally from Mexico. Combining these numbers, a conservative estimate of people of Mexican descent currently re-

Hispanic origin groups in the U.S., 2021

Origin group	Population	% among all U.S. Hispanics	% change 2010-2021
U.S. total	62,530,000	100%	23%
Mexican	37,235,000	59.5	13
Puerto Rican	5,800,000	9.3	24
Salvadoran	2,475,000	4.0	35
Cuban	2,400,000	3.8	28
Dominican	2,395,000	3.8	59
Guatemalan	1,770,000	2.8	53
Colombian	1,400,000	2.2	46
Honduran	1,150,000	1.8	57
Spaniard	995,000	1.6	43
Ecuadorian	815,000	1.3	25
Peruvian	720,000	1.2	20
Venezuelan	660,000	1.1	172
Nicaraguan	455,000	0.7	19
Argentinean	295,000	0.5	26
Panamanian	240,000	0.4	37
Costa Rican	190,000	0.3	44
Chilean	190,000	0.3	35
Bolivian	130,000	0.2	15
Uruguayan	65,000	0.1	9
Paraguayan	30,000	0.0	42
Other South American	40,000	0.1	62
Other Central American	30,000	0.0	1
All other Latinos	3,050,000	4.9	96

siding in the U.S. is at least sixty million. Despite declining birth rates in the U.S. since 2000, fertility is still highest among immigrant women. A Pew Research Center study from 2017 showed births per 1000 women ages 15 to 44, were 77.4 to foreign born and 56.2 to U.S. born women. In 2018, 50% of all births to foreign born women were to Latinas. In the U.S., the trend over the last decade has been the declining share of births to White non-Latino women. From 2000 to 2018, the percent of births for all women, U.S. born and foreign born, decreased from 59% to 53% to White women, while it increased from 20% to 24% to Latino women, and remained at 15% to Black women. In 2020, the U.S. General Fertility Rates per 1000 women ages 15-44 were 53.2 to White non-Latino women, 59.2 to Black non-Latino women, and 63.1 to Latino women. Interestingly, in 2019 and 2020, for the first time in U.S. history, women ages 30-34 had the highest fertility rates, surpassing those aged 25-29. Since about two thirds of Latino women are born in the U.S., these trends indicate Latino women, like other ethnic groups in the U.S., are waiting to complete their studies, acquire a skill set, including technical training, and get married, all prior to having children. Many have learned from their parents' struggles, who may have arrived in the U.S. without completing high school or higher education, worked in manual labor and service industries, and are instead choosing to take advantage of the opportunities their parents and the U.S. offer. Among U.S. born women, from 2000 to 2018, the share of all births decreased to White mothers from 71% to 63%, Latinas increased from 10% to 17%, and Blacks stayed at 17%. Lastly, according to the CDC, in 2020, the total fertility rates (lifetime live births) per 1000 women in the U.S., were 1,875.5 for Latinas, 1,714 for Blacks, 1,552 for non-Latino Whites, and 1,385 for Asians. These statistics indicate that Latinos will continue to have the highest fertility rates and the anticipated population growth for the foreseeable decades in the U.S. The recent record-breaking international migration will further accentuate such trends.

The predominant provenance of these Latinos is no longer Mexico, but instead from Central American countries, Venezuela, and the Dominican Republic. Latinos are a diverse group, each with its unique history, culture, customs, and linguistic nuances. Assimilation and integration to U.S. society represents a different challenge for each group, mostly depending on educational level, skill sets, prior training, proficiency in English, other family already in the U.S., and individual migratory status as economic migrant versus refuge asylum seeker. Thus far in U.S. history Latinos have not been a united group. Various national coalitions since the 1930s and 1960s have attempted to create a country-wide Latino coalition, especially for political leverage, initially attempting to include the largest groups, those of Mexican descent, Puerto Ricans, and Cubans. Over the decades, the results of such laudable efforts and initiatives have not resulted in a unified Latino front. This in part is indicative of Latino diversity. Latinos from different countries and even within each nation, have a different genetic make-up derived from the diverse indigenous populations that spread in waves throughout the Americas more than fifteen thousand years ago. To these separate groups, we must add over the last five hundred years different peoples from Spain and other European nations, Africa, Middle East, and more recently from Asia. The different mix in each subsequent nation undoubtedly resulted in the various unique present and past civilizations and cultures in Latin America and the Caribbean. The Aztecs and Incas, among others, may have been conquered, or as in the case of the Mayans which declined for diverse reasons not exactly known, still have millions of surviving ancestors that form part of current nations. Most Latin countries have a predominance of indigenous or mixed race European with native peoples, whereas several have a mostly European-derived population. Our distinct histories, cultures, language differences and educational levels, and, just as importantly, the historical lack of a national unifying voice or trusted individuals, have prevented Latinos from becoming a "Pan Latino Bloc," especially in the U.S. political arena. Is there a real possibility that it may one day such a coalition become a reality, especially as more educated, meritorious, and visionary Latinos penetrate the highest levels of the political landscape?

LATINOS OR HISPANICS AND LATINX

Since almost two-thirds of Latinos are born in the U.S., they are like other Americans and frequently only have passing knowledge of their ancestor's nation of origin. These growing Latino groups, mostly young and English-speaking individuals, have significant diversity from their own ancestors, which inevitably widens from generation to generation. So, should they be called Latinos or Hispanics? Or Latin Americans or simply Americans?

The history of Hispanic and Latino terminology started during the Nixon administration, when in the 1970s, mostly for political expediency, the term Hispanic was used to identify a group that had been overlooked and needed representation. The U.S. Census Bureau first placed the term on the 1980 census. Hispanic was defined as any person who descended from a Spanish speaking country, including people in Spain and others in the U.S. who grew up speaking Spanish at home. Although the term Hispanic became widely accepted, in the 1990s it related to Spanish colonialism and various atrocities committed against native populations throughout the Americas and Caribbean. This led to the term Latino as a replacement. Latino refers to those who descend from Latin America, regardless of their language of origin, excluding people from Spain. By this definition, as an example, Portuguese-speaking Brazilians are considered Latin Americans. Currently in the U.S., as noted above, there is a diverse population of people who identify as Latinos, each from a different nation of origin, each with unique cultural, political, and language traditions. Most people in the U.S. use these terms, Hispanic and Latino, interchangeably. For the purposes of this book, I have used the term Latino since most of the topics included in this work exclude Spaniards. Also, the title, *The Latin Century*, rolls better off the tongue!

The recent use of the term Latinx to describe a person of Latin American origin or descent, as an alternative to Latino or Latina, has created some controversy, especially among Latinos. It is meant to be more inclusive as a gender-neutral or nonbinary alternative to the traditional gender-based Spanish language that labels objects and living organisms as male or female. Latinx was created by English-speaking queer Latinos in the early 2000s, first appearing in 2004 Google trends. The rationale for its use was the highlighting of intersectionality by applying the letter "X" and the feminist movement's rejection of defaulting to a masculine term, so common in the gender-based Spanish language. The letter "X" also had ties to the Chicano and Civil Rights movements of the 1960s. In the 2010s the term Latinx gradually gained acceptance to describe pan-ethnic, gender-inclusive people. Indigenous peoples have rejected the term since it is a reminder of the fact colonists forced the letter "X" into languages during the conquest. Currently, critics say the term does not fit traditional Spanish grammar, it violates conventional Spanish, and it is unnatural and difficult to pronounce. According to a 2020 Pew Research Center survey, only three percent of Latin Americans use the term. A 2021 Gallup poll found four percent accepted the term. A November 2021 poll conducted by Miami-based Bendixen and Amandi International, found some forty percent of U.S. born Latin Americans are offended by the term Latinx and only two percent identify as Latinx. Older Latinos, especially foreign-born, reject the term altogether, preferring to identify as Hispanics or Latinos and according to their ancestors' nation of origin. The League of United Latin American Citizens (LULAC), the oldest Latino civil rights organization in the U.S., dropped the term since it was so rejected by most Latinos. Recently, some politicians, including U.S. President Biden, media personalities, liberal academics, and progressives, have used the term during election campaign speeches, local presentations, and various cable network, legacy, and social media platforms, even though there is almost complete dislike of the term by the very people they are attempting to reach. In fact, the irony is that instead of more inclusivity, for most Latinos or

Hispanics, Latinx erases a vital part of their language and identity, replacing it with an English word. Language purists point to the fact that Latin is several thousand years old, with its various gender-based romantic language offspring, including Italian, French, Portuguese, and Spanish, which should all be respected and celebrated, and not violated by an English word that interjects gender ideology. In this narrative, when applicable, I will continue to use the gender-based Spanish.

PEW RESEARCH CENTER | OCTOBER 7, 2022

KEY FACTS ABOUT HISPANIC ELIGIBLE VOTERS IN 2022

Hispanic eligible voter population projected to exceed 34.5 million in 2022, up almost 5 million from 2018

Hispanic eligible voter population projected to exceed 34.5 million in 2022, up almost 5 million from 2018

U.S. eligible voter population change, by race and ethnicity, 2018-2022

	2022 EV pop.	EV pop. change, 2018-22	% change in EV pop., 2018-22
Hispanic	34,550,000	4,700,000	16%
Black	32,700,000	750,000	2%
Asian	13,350,000	1,050,000	9%
Total	241,300,000	7,650,000	3%

POLITICS, VOTING, AND LATINOS

According to the Pew Research Center, in 2008 Latinos were 9.2% or 19.3 million of U.S. eligible voters. In 2018 these numbers were 12.8% and 29.9 million of the electorate. The 2022 numbers were 14.3% and 34.55 million people. These numbers represent a 16% increase in eligible voters in just four years and reflect a critical pattern likely to continue during each subsequent four-year time frame. For the first time in U.S. history, Latinos eligible to vote in 2022 surpassed Blacks (13.5% and 32.7 million), with 53% of the total Latino population now eligible to vote. By 2035 Latinos eligible to vote will be close to 50 million people. Certainly, in future election cycles, with the projected growth in the Latino population for each decade of the twenty-first century far outpacing all other racial groups, Latinos will play an increasingly greater role in deciding local, state, and federal elections. If one also considers the rapidly growing Latino GDP contribution to the U.S. economy, the fact is that as a group, even with each member of the Latino coalition's unique characteristics, public office seekers will not have the luxury of neglecting, ignoring, gas-lighting, or pandering to Latinos, especially with inauthentic altruism, as has been the historical pattern. Each Latino group has its own priorities, mostly based on their cultural background, particular idiosyncrasies, and specific desires that candidates need to genuinely first understand and act on, rather than simple, one-size-fits-all general promises that will likely remain unfulfilled. It is easy to comprehend why Latinos were politically largely ignored in the nineteenth and twentieth centuries. For the most part, during each election cycle, especially mid-term elections, Latinos represented a relatively small numbers of the overall electorate with poor registration and participation numbers, far less than Whites and Blacks. Optimistically, in recent election cycles, both mid-terms and federal presidential elections have demonstrated increasing participation by diverse Latino groups. This is a trend that is likely to continue.

HISTORICAL ELECTION OVERVIEW

On the eve of the tight 1960 presidential campaign, then candidate John F. Kennedy turned to an often-overlooked group for support: Latinos. After all, he was Catholic, as they were too. Until then largely ignored by political candidates, with a total population of about 3.5 million people, mostly of Mexican descent, any edge Mr. Kennedy might secure could put him in the White House. The simple yet complicated goal was to unite all Latinos into one voting bloc. With Puerto Ricans living mostly in the Northeast, Cubans in Florida, and Mexicans in the Southwest, the task would at best prove difficult. After all, these distinct groups had distinct political and cultural roots, mostly based on where they or their ancestors had migrated from. Cuban refugees were at the time recent arrivals who expected to soon overthrow the usurper Fidel Castro and return to their homeland. Due to all this diversity, most Latinos did not act as if they were attached to a political party, nor did they share a vision of a common Latino community. The most numerous by far were Mexicans, many of whom could trace their ancestry to the seventeenth century, long before there was a United States of America. The Kennedy campaign pondered if at least the Mexicans and Puerto Ricans could be unified into a single constituency, even a national alliance, to vote for their candidate. For well-meaning, ambitious Mexican Americans, this was an opportunity. A liberal councilman from Los Angeles, Edward Roybal, soon became the leader in uniting the Latino vote. This was what became known as the "Viva Kennedy" campaign to awaken the Mexican vote, mostly in Texas. The expectation was that once President Kennedy took office, there would be a reciprocal initiative to implement federal resources to improve Latino economic and social conditions as well as important federal jobs and influence in state and national Democratic Party positions for the leaders.

Roybal and his group quickly mobilized throughout the country forming "Viva Kennedy" clubs which served as direct connections between their communities and the candidate. This was clearly a way for Latinos, mostly Mexican Americans, to start participating in mainstream national politics. Soon Puerto Rican leaders joined the effort, creating an optimism among Latinos that they no longer needed to deny their identity and heritage, but instead to know they would be an important voice in the present and future elections. JFK spoke in New York to large groups of Puerto Ricans and in Los Angeles to different groups of Mexican Americans. The excitement for the candidate was palpable. The sentiment was that JFK was an outsider, a Catholic in a predominantly protestant nation, just like they were. When Kennedy won, some in California, which had gone Republican, said that

Kennedy had ridden the Mexican burro to the White House. In 1960, 68.8 million people voted, with the non-white vote being 10.1%, most of them Blacks. The Latino vote had been miniscule at best, or about 2.1% of the total vote. Once in the White House, not surprisingly, the predictable occurred. The administration neglected the "Viva Kennedy" campaign promises, and in particular pledges made to Mexican Americans. There were to be no federal positions or considerations for any of the "Viva Kennedy" campaigners. The "national" coalition between Mexicans and Puerto Ricans quickly disintegrated. Unfortunately, this would foster general apathy, mostly among Mexican Americans, about the futility of registering and voting in future presidential elections.

In 1970 the Census Bureau data reported the total Latino population in the U.S. at 9.1 million. In the 1972 presidential election, out of a total voting age population (VAP) of 140.5 million, Latinos were only 5.6 million. Out of these, 44.4% registered to vote and eventually 2.1 million voted or only 37% of the VAP. These numbers were vastly inferior to the 78.2 million Whites and 7.0 million Blacks who voted, or 64.5% and 52.1% respectively of their VAP. This was not surprising given the minimal effort put forth by both Republican and Democratic campaigns to attract the Latino vote. For many Latinos language had played a role since voting materials were not available in Spanish. This matter would not be corrected until 1975 with an amendment of the Voting Rights Act of 1965 that attempted to prevent voting discrimination against members of "language minority groups."

In 1976 the total U.S. VAP was 150.8 million people and 88.2 million voted. Of these, only 2.1 million Latinos voted or about 31.8% of the 6.6 million VAP, constituting only 2.4% of the total votes cast. Once again, Latinos showed up at the polls at an inferior percentage than Whites (60.9%) and Blacks (48.7%). This same pattern would continue in 1980, when the total

Latino population according to the Census Bureau was 14.6 million. The VAP for the U.S. was 162.3 million and the total number of votes cast was 94.6 million. Of the 8.2 million VAP Latinos, 2.45 million voted or 29.9%. Once again, a far inferior number than the 88.9 million Whites and 8.3 million Blacks who voted, or 60.9% and 50.5% respectively. The Latino vote represented only about 2.5% of the total vote.

In 1984, Latinos participated slightly more, on account of promises of an amnesty program that would be eventually approved by President Ronald Raegan's administration in 1986 (the Immigration Reform Control Act). This resulted in some 2.7 million people (about the population of Mississippi) being granted permanent residence. The total number of votes cast was 103.5 million out of a VAP of 174.7 million. Latinos cast 3.1 million votes or 32.6% of the 9.5 million VAP. The issue continued to be the low registration rate also seen in prior elections, this time at 40.1%. The Latino vote was a mere 3% of the total vote and yet it was the highest participation to date. Poor registration and turnout on election day continued to be the pattern. By comparison, Whites voted at 61.4% and Blacks at 55.8% of VAP. Since more than two-thirds of Latinos were Mexican Americans, it was evident some continued to feel their voice and vote would not matter, despite the promise of an imminent amnesty program for undocumented friends and family.

Subsequent presidential elections in 1988, 1992, and 1996 had a minimal increase in rates of Latino registration and election participation. Latinos cast 4.0%, 4.05% and 5.1% of the total votes for each of these three elections. The overall percentage was 28.8%, 28.9%, and 26.7% of the VAP. During the same elections Whites and Blacks voted at greater than 50% of their respective VAPs. During those years, the Latino VAP grew from 12.9 million to 18.4 million, yet election participation continued to lag.

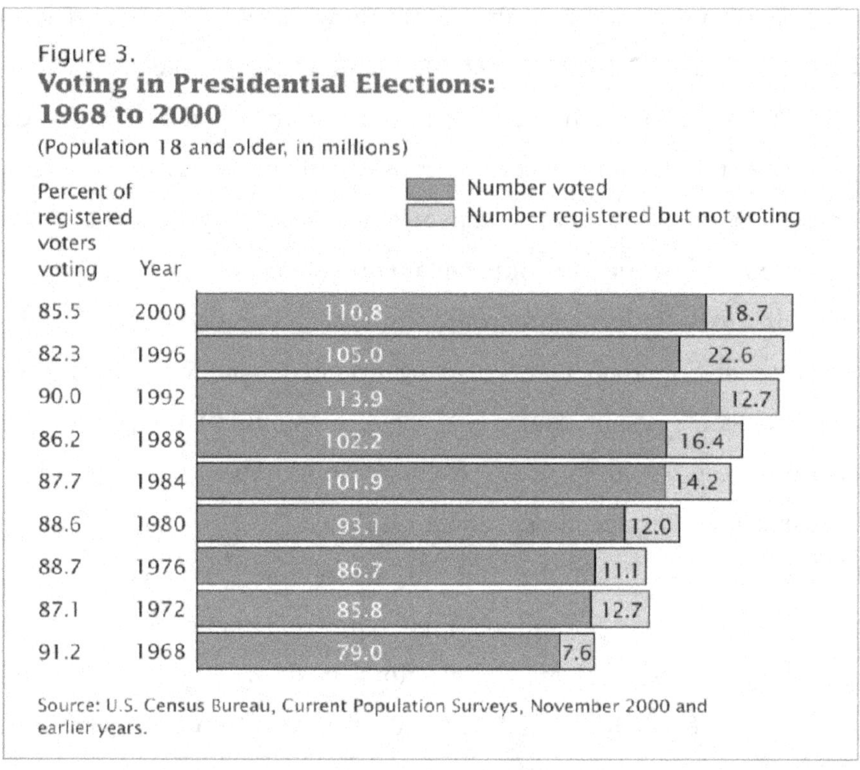

From the 2008 to the 2020 presidential elections, the Latino vote gradually increased from 7% to 10% of total votes cast. In 2020, out of 158.3 million votes, Whites cast 113.9 million (72%), Blacks 18.9 million (12%), and Latinos 15.8 million (10%). This represented a significant increase in Latino election registration and participation from prior years, at about 49% of the eligible 32.3 million voters (about twice the population of New York). This signaled a Latino population, with about two-thirds born in the U.S., more invested in the political landscape, each group with its own priorities such as opposition to socialist policies, dissatisfaction with the defund the police movement, demands for immigration re-form, better educational and employment opportunities, safer neighborhoods and anti-crime strategies, a cogent Covid-19 pandemic policy, and respect for family values and faith. Given the acrimonious campaigns by both political parties in 2020, fueled by a polarized mainstream media, Latinos experienced the daily hate and fear fueled politicians, mainstream media, including Spanish language networks, and social media "big tech" companies.

Composition of the Electorate by Race, 2008-2020

Race	2008	2012	2016	2020	2016 to 2020
White	77%	75%	74%	72%	-2.0%
Black	12%	13%	12%	12%	-0.1%
Latino	7%	7%	9%	10%	+1.2%
Asian	3%	3%	4%	4%	+0.8%
Other	1%	1%	2%	2%	+0.1%
White Non-College	51%	48%	46%	44%	-1.6%
White College	26%	27%	28%	28%	-0.4%

vox.com

More Hispanics than non-Hispanics say the U.S. government is doing too little to protect environment

% who say the federal government is doing too little to ...

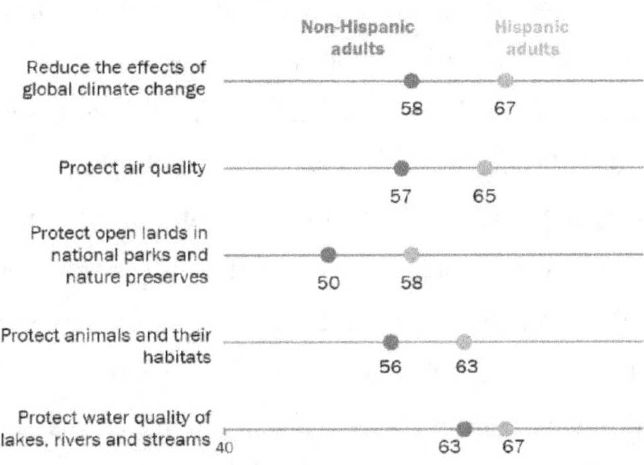

Note: Shares of respondents saying each issue is not a problem or who did not offer an answer not shown. Hispanics are of any race.
Source: Survey of U.S. adults conducted April 20-29, 2021

PEW RESEARCH CENTER

2022 MID-TERM ELECTION

The recent 2022 mid-term election continued the recent trend of increasing Latino participation. This is due to several factors, including the larger number of U.S.-born Latinos, more awareness about the importance of their vote and voice in the political arena, and higher educational levels. In 2022, Latinos clearly demonstrated diverse priorities when they cast their ballots. The top five were (1) inflation and the cost of living, (2) crime and gun violence, (3) jobs and the economy, (4) healthcare, and (5) abortion. Despite of traditional conservative values, including their deep-rooted Christian faith, some 75% want abortion to be legal. Another critical issue is the environment. Interestingly, more foreign-born than U.S. born Latinos are concerned about the environment. For many Latinos, mostly those of Mexican descent living in states adjacent to the U.S.-Mexico border, immigration policy is a high priority issue. These are genuine issues politicians must seriously consider, fully understanding that within the various Latino communities some issues have a higher priority.

Latino voters in 2022 continued to vote for Democrats. There were about 34.5 million Latinos eligible to vote. There was a total of 104.1 million votes cast in these mid-term elections. The anticipated "red wave" never materialized, except in Florida. However, nationally, there was a subtle shift towards the Republican camp, a trend noted since 2018 when 32% of Latinos voted Republican. In 2022 the number was 39%. The fundamental issues influencing the vote were noted above. The Florida results were the most impressive in that 58% of Latinos voted for the Republican governor, and 55% for the Republican Senator. By heritage, Republicans were favored by Cubans (67%), Puerto Ricans (54%) and other Latinos greater than 50%. By age all favored Republicans except the 18–29-year-old group (39%) and by gender (male 55%, female 57%) also Republican. Some long-standing

Democrat counties, such as Miami-Dade, flipped Republican by eleven points for the first time in more than twenty years. The most critical issue for Latinos in Florida was inflation and the cost of living. The major factor in Florida for the "red wave" was the performance of the sitting Governor Ron DeSantis. His management of the Covid-19 pandemic, the successful stand against the "woke agenda" at Disney and in school curriculums, prevention of crime strategies by supporting police officers, his management of hurricane Ian, confrontation of the mainstream media, among others, all contributed to his high popularity. In Texas, with Governor Abbott re-elected, Democrats lost some ground since they won Latino majority counties by 7%, down by 3% from 2020. Just as in Florida, the 18–29-year-old group voted 76% Democrat, with 35% of all Latino voters stating abortion was the main issue. Texas' current stand on abortion appears problematic. Nationally, Republicans did not perform as well as had been predicted, even though they did take a slim majority in the House of Representatives. Latinos have been gradually shifting ever so slowly towards the Republican side. As the Latino electorate continues to grow, it cannot be ignored or simply taken for granted. Both parties will need to refocus on the various issues important to the diverse Latino communities, each with their own priorities.

PROJECTION FOR THE 2024 ELECTION

It is estimated that there will be some 40 million eligible Latino voters in the 2024 Presidential election. In the 2020 election, Latinos comprised ten percent of the total vote or approximately 15.8 million votes. This was in part due to increased turnout from 2016 by thirty-one percent. The trend is likely to continue in 2024. If that is the case, plus the growing electorate of young Latinos, millions who will be aging up to voting eligibility, it is some twelve to fourteen percent of the total vote will be cast by Latinos, or about twenty million votes. The question is whether Latinos will continue to support Democrat politicians, given the situation at the end of 2022. The strategies employed in 2023 by the slight majority Republican Congress and the current Democrat administration, especially in the management of the five key issues of concern noted above, will be critical, as for other racial groups as well. For Latinos, as for most of the country, there are serious concerns about the current direction of the country. These include the border crisis, immigration policy, public education academic standards, and foreign policy expenditures on the war in Ukraine. Since most economic and financial experts are conceding a worldwide recession for 2023 and 2024, the next twelve to eighteen months' handling of the above issues by those in power will determine how far Latinos will continue to gradually drift Republican, as has been the case since 2016. A further five to ten percent shift may make a significant difference in the popular vote and in several key states. A similar trend was observed in the Black population vote in these recent mid-term elections. In 2020, ninety percent of Blacks voted Democrat. In the 2022 mid-term election, eighty-three percent voted Democrat, but in the key demographic of 18–44-year-olds, the number was fifty-four percent. These are not positive trends for Democrats, who have traditionally depended on a large Black and Latino minority vote.

Latinos are frustrated about inflation and the cost of living, especially energy and food prices, which they increasingly view as based on ideological policies to rapidly transition to renewable energies prematurely, as affordable technologies that replace fossil fuels are not yet available. Latinos in the U.S., as most in Latin America, except for administrations in Cuba, Venezuela, and Nicaragua, are against the invasion of Ukraine by Russia. They heavily favor diplomatic resolutions. Where there is a split, is on how much economic support the U.S. can afford to keep sending to Ukraine and for how long, especially with the highest inflation in forty years and a struggling U.S. economy. Latinos also understand, given the current high interest rates, the housing market will take a heavy toll in 2023, eroding their main source of household wealth. Ignoring such serious matters will have a definitive impact on the 2024 federal elections.

Two-Way (Democrat vs. Republican) Support for Democratic Candidates, 2012-2020

Race	2012	2016	2020	2016 to 2020
White	42%	41%	44%	+3%
Black	97%	93%	90%	-3%
Latino	70%	71%	63%	-8%
Asian	66%	68%	67%	-1%
Other	55%	53%	55%	+2%
White Non-College	40%	36%	37%	+1%
White College	46%	50%	54%	+4%

It is evident that since 2016 Republicans have done a better job at reaching middle-class and working-class voters. However, the results in 2024 will depend on who is nominated as the Republican candidate. At the end of 2022, the front runners are ex-President Donald Trump and Governor Ron DeSantis. Others may emerge in the next twelve months. It appears, given the fact that a "red wave" did not occur in 2022, and the senate will remain under Democrat control, President Joe Biden is poised to run for re-election. An extremely tight race is anticipated unless the issues are not significantly improved or resolved by the current administration. If that is the case, then here is a prediction. If some 160 million people vote in the 2024 Presidential election, with approximately 112 million Whites and 48 million minorities casting a ballot, the estimated popular vote results will be:

- Whites ~ 57% Republican, 43% Democrat.
  Votes: 63,840,000 R and 48,160,000 D.
- Blacks ~ 68% Democrat, 32% Republican.
  Votes: 13,056,000 D and 6,144,000 R
- Latinos ~ 55% Democrat, 45% Republican.
  Votes: 10,560,000 D and 8,640,000 R
- Asians ~ 55% Democrat, 45% Republican
  Votes: 3,520,000 D and 2,880,000 R
- Other ~ 60% Democrat, 40% Republican
  Votes: 1,920,000 D and 1,280,000 R

Total Votes: R 82,784,000 and D 77,216,000

This prediction on the popular vote for the 2024 presidential election may at first seem surprising. But if one considers the current progressive Democratic Party agenda, the present U.S. economy, inflation, illegal immigration, other border issues, recent voting trends by Blacks, all coupled with traditional Latino conservative values and priorities when casting ballots, it is likely the popular vote will continue to drift to Republican Party candidates. Although much will depend on the final nominees for president, at this moment, especially with control of the House of Representatives, if these leaders perform their duties responsibly in addressing the needs of the population over the next two years, more likely than not, Republicans stand to win the popular vote.

ECONOMY, EDUCATION, AND LATINOS

According to the Peter G. Peterson Foundation (PGPF), the U.S.
median household income in 2020 was $67,521. This was about $2000 less
than 2019, reflecting the first year of the Covid-19 pandemic, which
contributed to a drop in income for all groups. The household income in 2020
varied significantly by race and ethnicity with Asians at $94,903, Whites at
$74,912, Latinos at $55,321, and Blacks at $45,870. In addition, the 2019
Survey of Consumer Finances by the Board of Governors of the Federal
Reserve System reported the household net worth for each race. Whites were
at $181,440, Latinos at $36,180, Blacks at $20,730, and Others at $193,700.
In households with the head of family only completing a high school
education, the values were: Whites at $113,970, Latinos at $50,600, Blacks at
$15,700, and Others at $15,150 (see tables on next page). These values speak

loudly to the fact that the most successful group of people in the U.S. continue to be Asians, but also that level of education matters.

The above numbers on the significant racial differences in both median household income and net worth are staggering. However, these must be examined through the lens of educational status to draw more accurate conclusions beyond race and ethnicity. According to PGPF, in 2020 the median household income for those with a bachelor's degree or more was $106,936, an associate degree $68,769, high school or equivalent $29,520 and less than ninth grade $29,609. Education status clearly divides Americans into clear cut income brackets. Given the racial and educational differences, where do Latinos stand in comparison to the other groups? Are Latinos catching up on college education and graduation rates?

In 2020, median household income varied considerably by race and ethnicity

Race/Ethnicity of Household Head	2019 Median Household Income (2020 dollars)	2020 Median Household Income (2020 dollars)
All races/ethnicities	$69,560	$67,521
Asian	$99,400	$94,903
White, not Hispanic	$77,007	$74,912
Hispanic (any race)	$56,814	$55,321
Black	$46,005	$45,870

Median household income varies based on the educational attainment of the household head

Educational Attainment of Household Head	2020 Median Household Income
All education levels	$69,228
Less than 9th grade	$29,609
Some high school	$29,520
High school or equivalent	$47,405
Some college, no degree	$60,392
Associate degree	$68,769
Bachelor's degree or more	$106,936

SOURCE: United States Census Bureau, Current Population Survey, 2020 and 2021 Annual Social and Economic Supplements.
NOTE: The differences between the values above are not all statistically significant at the confidence level used by the Census Bureau.

© 2021 Peter G. Peterson Foundation

SOURCE: United States Census Bureau, Current Population Survey, 2020 and 2021 Annual Social and Economic Supplements.

© 2021 Peter G. Peterson Foundation

According to the Pew Research Center, in 2021 the percent of 18–24-year-olds enrolled in college or who have a bachelor's degree were 58% of Asians, 37% of Whites, 33% of Blacks and 32% of Latinos. Those 25–29-year-olds enrolled in college were 72% of Asians, 45% of Whites, 26% of Blacks and 23% of Latinos. The younger group of Latinos is enrolling at a higher percentage. These statistics align with the observation that median household income is proportional to education status. Interestingly, also according to the Pew Research Center, about 70% of Latinos without a bachelor's degree cite cost of education and the need to support a family for not obtaining such degrees. About 47% of Latinos state they did not want such a degree, 43% just did not consider it, and 41% felt they did not need more education for the job or career they wanted (See table).

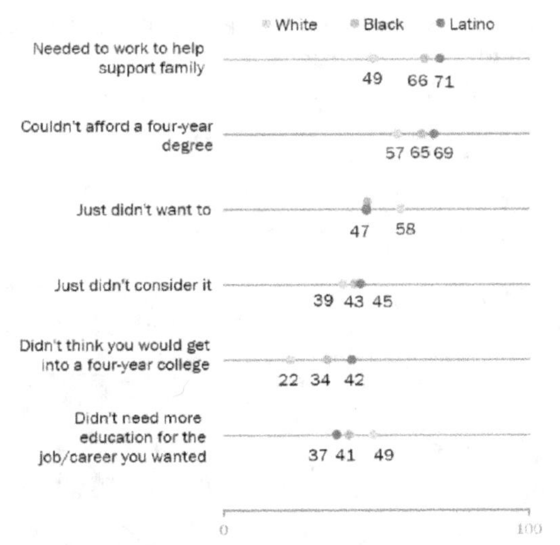

About seven-in-ten Latinos without a bachelor's degree cite a need to support family, cost as reasons why

Among adults who do not have a bachelor's degree and are not enrolled in school, % saying each is a major or minor reason they did not receive a four-year degree

Note: White and Black adults are single-race and not Latino. Latinos are of any race. Data for Asian adults is not shown due to small sample size.
Source: Pew Research Center Survey of U.S. adults conducted Oct. 18-24, 2021.

PEW RESEARCH CENTER

The reality is that Latinos in the twenty-first century have a tremendously bright future in the U.S. as far as education and household income are concerned. Why do I say that? If we accept that income is directly proportional to higher education, then consider these additional facts from the Pew Research Center: Latinos in 2020 made up 20% of all enrolled at postsecondary institutions. In 1980 it was 4%, in 1990 6%, in

Hispanic and Black Americans among the least likely to be enrolled in college or have a bachelor's degree

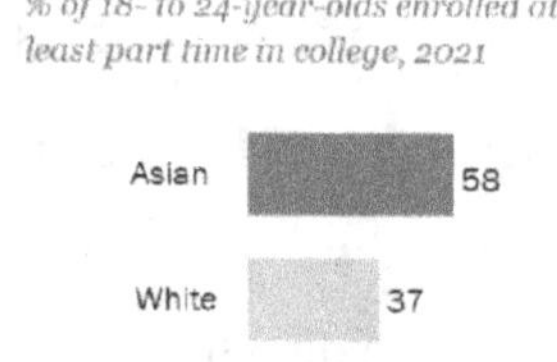

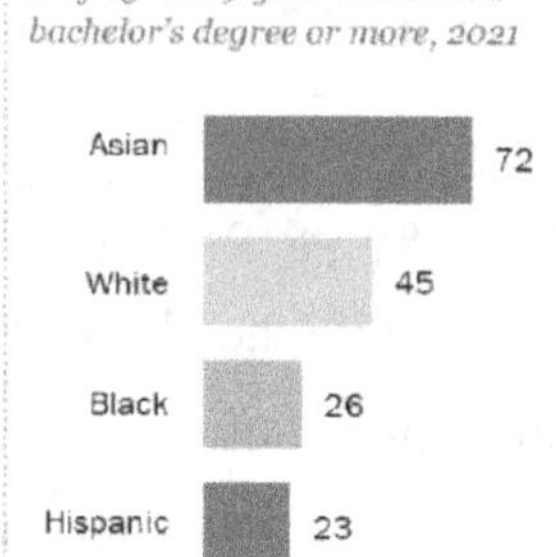

Note: White, Black and Asian adults are single-race and not Hispanic. Hispanics are of any race.
Source: Pew Research Center analysis of the March 2021 Current Population Survey Annual Social and Economic Supplement (IPUMS).

PEW RESEARCH CENTER

2000 10% and in 2010 14%. In 2020, 3.7 million Latinos students were enrolled with 2.4 million in four-year institutions and 1.3 million in two-year colleges (See table). In comparison, the percent of enrolled students in higher education by race from 1980 to 2020 demonstrate Asians have increased from 2% to 8%, Blacks from 9% to 13%, while Whites have decreased from 84% to 54% (see table). Between 2000 and 2020 the number of Latinos enrolled at four-year institutions grew from 620,000 to 2.4 million, a dramatic 287% increase, far outpacing all other groups which saw about a 50% growth. Latinos have clearly experienced a 40-forty-year catch-up phenomenon in enrollment at university and college institutions. Will this

Hispanics now make up one-in-five students enrolled at postsecondary institutions in the U.S.

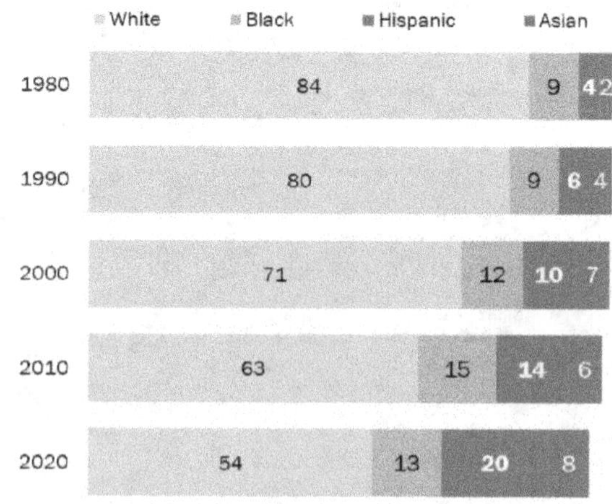

Note: Enrollment includes students of all ages. Asians include Pacific Islanders. Other races (not shown) include American Indian/Alaska Native and students with two or more races. White, Black and Asian students are single-race and not Hispanic. Hispanics are of any race. Nonresident students are not included in this analysis.
Source: National Center for Education Statistics, U.S. Department of Education

PEW RESEARCH CENTER

pattern continue? The likely answer to this question is yes. Multiple factors play a role in this phenomenon.

Of the approximate sixty-five million Latino population in 2022, two-thirds were born in the U.S. These individuals are U.S. citizens, completely assimilated to U.S. society, most speak English fluently, with 91% proficient in English in 2019, and now are aware that diverse educational opportunities exist to acquire marketable skills and if they so desire, two-year and four-year college degrees. Some initially enroll in a junior college program and then for the last two years transfer to a four-year university. Many such students qualify for various scholarship programs and loans. In fact, during the 2015-16 academic year, 76% of full time Latino students received some type of federal aid, while 67% of Whites, 50% of Asians, and 88% of Blacks were given such support. Some 60% of Latino students received a Pell Grant. Although the cost of higher education is significant, a topic recently covered by the mainstream media, increasingly Latinos are finding pathways to cover such tuition, including programs that offer work-study curricula. Present and future political candidates, and other office holders at state and federal levels, will need to prioritize the issue of college and university education cost in the U.S. It is imperative for bipartisan congressional lawmakers to find policies and strategies that effectively lower tuition costs in both private and public institutions. Also, more high school students need to first value the investment they are making in their education by enrolling in a field that will provide them with marketable degrees, thereby avoiding unemployment and the hardship of repaying loans. Unfortunately, many select courses and degrees in areas that do not have a clear path to a successful professional career in a technologically evolving free market economy. This is a current hot topic and will be a critical issue for most young voters in upcoming elections, including Latinos.

GROWING YOUNG POPULATION

The population growth that is forthcoming over the next three decades, as was stated previously, will result in a near tripling of Latinos graduating from high school and desiring higher education, once again outpacing all other racial and ethnic groups. It is a numbers game. Latinos are likely to reach 25% and up to 30% of all college and university enrollments in the following ten to fifteen years. Currently the median age of Latinos in the U.S. is twenty-eight. About 48% of Latinas have children under eighteen. With more growing emphasis on education attainment, Latino parents will continue to sacrifice to provide opportunities for their children, especially higher education. That may be the case, but what about graduation rates? According to the Education Data Initiative, in 2020 the Latino five-year college graduation rate was 41.5% and the six-year rate was 51%. In comparison, Whites graduated at 62.2% and 59% respectively. Blacks had a five-year graduation rate of 40.5% and not surprisingly, Asians graduated at a 69.3% rate. From 2010 to 2021, the percentage of individuals aged 24 to 29 with a bachelor's degree or higher increased for all racial groups. It grew from 13% to 23% for Latinos, 39% to 45% for Whites, 19% to 26% for Blacks and 56% to 72% for Asians. In the U.S. in 2019, those with master's degrees and doctoral PhDs were 66.8% and 57.8% White, 16.5% and 16.7% Latino, 9.5% and 10.5% Black and 4.5% and 11.5% Asian. In 2020, Latin females, compared to Latin males, had earned more than 50% of all degrees earned by Latinos. All these statistics demonstrate tremendous advances in Latino higher education achievement which will gradually continue to narrow the gap with Whites and Asians.

FIRST IN THE FAMILY

The Latino first generation education status is rapidly growing. In the

2015-16 academic year, 44% of Latinos enrolled in higher education were the first in their family to attend college. In comparison, Whites were 22%, Blacks 34%, and Asians 29%. This highlights the recognition by Latinos of breaking away from prior traditional and cultural behaviors within families that had not emphasized the value of higher education. In time, more high school graduate Latinos will not be the first or only members of their family to attend college. Latinos more than ever are preferring to obtain higher education as a pathway to improve their standard of living.

THE AMERICAN DREAM

The concept of the American Dream is not lost on Latinos. Many first-generation individuals who continue to trace their roots to their country of origin, especially Mexicans, fully appreciate the abundant opportunities the U.S. economy and society offers to immigrants. In contrast to the life they had back in their homeland, these individuals are grateful for such opportunities, including for the ability to regularly provide financial support to family back home. In 2021, remittances to Mexico grew 27.1% from $40.6 billion to $51.6% billion, ranking as the third largest recipient in the world behind China and India. About 94.9% of these remittances were sent from the U.S. For individuals able to support family back in Mexico, this constitutes part of their American Dream. Latinos born in the U.S. are like any other citizen of any other racial group and ethnicity. They love their country. They recognize the U.S. as their home, the source of their family's wellbeing, where they obtain education, security, and have new avenues wide open for success and prosperity. Weather they choose technical careers or professional degrees, they understand that for them, the freedom to choose such a journey, raising their children along the way, is their very own American Dream.

LABOR FORCE PARTICIPATION

The Latino labor force participation has its history in a traditional culture of work ethic, self-reliance, and the deep-rooted responsibility of taking care of family. As previously mentioned, the Covid-19 pandemic

represents a clear example of the sacrifices made by Latinos, at great personal peril, to maintain many aspects of the U.S. economy productive. Oftentimes, Latino parents who may not have had educational opportunities, as also commonly occurs in the various Asian communities, make tremendous sacrifices to provide their children with a valuable education, so vital for eventual economic success. Currently, occupations with the highest Latino concentration are farming, fishing, and forestry (43%), building and grounds cleaning and maintenance (37.9%), construction and extraction (35.7%), food preparation and serving (27.3%), transportation and material moving (23.9%), and others such as automotive repair, home services, and landscaping. Countless others have acquired great skill sets as HVAC engineers, electricians, plumbers, commercial and residential painters, often providing a higher standard of living than their parents. While Latinos remain overrepresented in the service occupations, they now make up 10.7% of management employees, up from 5.2% in 2000. This growing management statistic will serve to influence many more Latinos who would have previously been satisfied with a high school diploma, or with an associate degree, to instead seek a bachelor's degree or even higher education as a pathway to the U.S. socioeconomic upper classes. According to the U.S. Department of Labor Blog, the number of Latino workers has grown from 10.7 million in 1990 to 29 million in 2020 and is projected to reach 35.9 million by 2030. By 2030, one out of five workers will be Latino. These are also younger, with a median age of 38.5 years, than non-Latinos whose median age is 42 years. In general, Latinos are projected to account for 78% of all new workers in the U.S. between 2020 and 2030. For many, college and university education, especially in STEM fields, will prepare them to gradually become, in greater numbers, an integral part of the upper management echelons of the U.S. labor force. It is safe to say, especially in service occupations, at this time in history Latinos have rapidly become the backbone of the U.S. labor force.

AFFIRMATIVE ACTION

The current case being argued at the Supreme Court is whether the affirmative-action program violates the Fourteenth Amendment of the constitution, which guarantees "to equal protection of the law." The question is what constitutes racial discrimination? The case against Harvard and the University of North Carolina is that these institutions discriminate against Asians, who on average have higher standardized test results than all other racial or ethnic groups, including Whites. In the past, Harvard had a Jewish quota, limiting their numbers, and today Asians represent Jews of the past. In fact, most Ivy League campuses from the 1920s to the 1960s severely limited Jews from admission, clearly a result of racist policies. In 2019, Harvard admitted some 1600 first-year students and had some 35,000 applicants. Of these, 2700 had perfect verbal SAT scores, 3700 had perfect math SAT scores, and more than 8000 had perfect GPAs. Asians constituted 28% of the

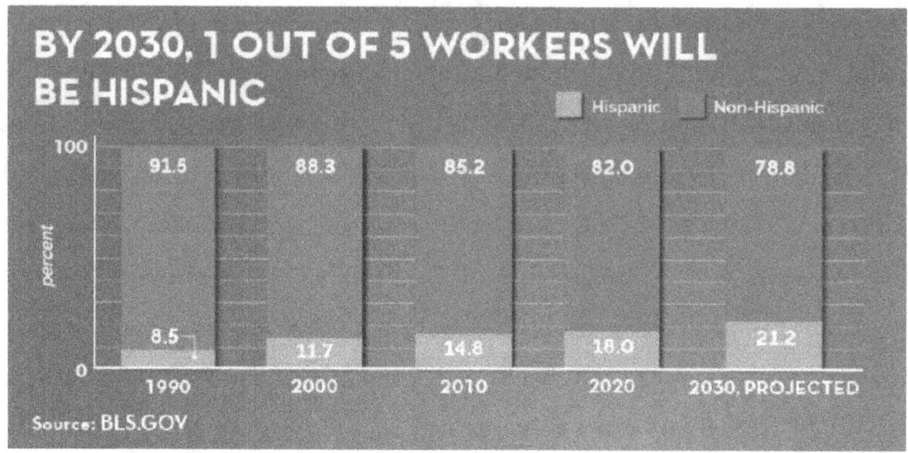

entering class while the U.S. Asian population is about 7.2%. The case argues that shortsighted affirmative action race-based admission policies discriminate against talented Asian and White students. The initial intent of preventing racism and admission discrimination against minorities such as Blacks, Latinos, and Native American Indians, was well intended. The argument was that these minorities were admittedly at a tremendous disadvantage for a variety of reasons that included socioeconomic factors, lower elementary and high school educational standards, and, at times, especially in Latino households, language and cultural barriers. In considering race as a determinant for admission to higher education institutions, the commonsense thinking was that the "playing field" would eventually level. The 1960s were a heady decade for Civil Rights, the war on poverty, and bigger government involvement if the lives of everyday Americans.

The question more than 50 years later is weather American universities should continue to use race as a criterion for admission, which gives certain minorities an unfair advantage. In 2003, Sandra Day O'Connor, Supreme Court Justice, stated, "We expect that twenty-five years from now, the use of racial preferences will no longer be necessary." At the time the court suggested that affirmative action's days were numbered. The well-meant sentiment was that a temporary aid to minorities would galvanize and inspire younger populations of students in minority communities to elevate academic proficiencies and standardized test scores. Unfortunately, this did not occur except for in isolated cases. One may then ask if affirmative action has had the intended benefits. Is affirmative action inherently unfair to Asians and Whites?

There are two main sides to these questions. On the one hand, should disad-

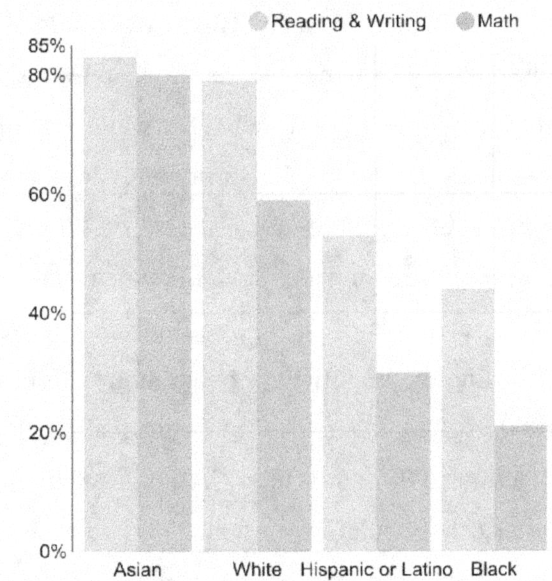

College Board, "SAT Suite of Assessments Annual Report," 2020.

BROOKINGS

vantaged minorities continue to get preferential entry to college and university campuses, based mostly on race, even when their GPAs and SAT scores are inferior to Asian and White applicants? Is this truly addressing racial discrimination in the twenty-first century? Or, instead, as many have pointed out, is affirmative action superficially treating a symptom of a much bigger problem? Plenty of data demonstrate that proficiency differences start early in elementary school on key subjects such as math, science, and English. These differences tend to widen in middle and high school, such that college-readiness benchmarks are not readily met by vast numbers of Latinos and Blacks. According to the Brookings Institute, college readiness in math, reading, and writing are significantly different by race. Approximately 80% or more of Asians meet these benchmarks, while 60% or more of Whites, Latinos at about 55%, and Blacks 45% or less, especially in math (see table). The facts on SAT math scores are that 43% of Asians and 45% of Whites are at the top of the score distribution, while only 6% of Latinos and 1% of Blacks join them at the top. Not surprisingly, at the bottom of the SAT math score distribution is 2% of Asians, 23% of Whites, 43% of Latinos and 26% of Blacks. Despite a wide range of strategies since the mid-1990s, the race-gap SAT score distribution by 2020 has scarcely narrowed. Interestingly, reflecting the important population growth in the Latino communities, from 2000 to 2020, the number of Latinos taking the SAT rose 482%, by 119% in Blacks, and 28% in Whites. In fact, SAT participation by Latinos has grown faster than population growth. This pattern points to Latino students' desire, for the vast majority of those born in the U.S., for higher education as a pathway forward to socioeconomic middle-and upper-class status.

The reality is that recent statistics indicate that affirmative action race-based college and university admission policies may in fact have had an undesirable impact on minorities they were meant to elevate. According to the Brookings Institute, the four-year college graduation rates by race are about 50% for Asians, 45% of Whites, 32% of Latinos and 21% of Blacks. The five- and six-year graduation rates, as noted previously, also lag for Latinos and Blacks. Many more Latinos and Blacks are not college ready, with lower SAT scores, especially in math, creating a self-fulfilling prophesy. The realization that a "crutch" was applied to allow them in, resulting in feelings of inferiority and debilitating doubt. When these students falter academically, they come to feel they are not supposed to do as well as Asians and Whites, and that they may not belong at such institutions. In addition, students with excellent academic merit who were denied admission to various high-ranking institutions by these policies become despondent, angry, and feel discriminated against. Simply stating that they "did not interview well," as has been the case with some deserving Asian students, has been a frequently employed tactic to deny talented Asians admission to various high-ranking institutions. Also, many disadvantaged Whites have come to feel discriminated against, to the extent that they leave blank the box that designates race, believing it would push them to the back of the affirmative action line. Many minority students admitted to colleges and universities via affirmative action race-based policies inevitably experience on-campus racial tensions as their status is questioned and even ridiculed. These issues help explain the inordinate dropout rates of those minorities admitted by affirmative action race-preference policies.

As early as 2005, the Educational Evaluation and Policy Analysis published evidence from the University of California at San Diego indicating the difference in graduation rates of affirmative action students was 57%, versus non-affirmative action students was 73%. On average the first group earned lower GPAs by 0.30. Their analysis determined that pre-college academic preparation explained most of the difference. Similar observations were noted at the prestigious University of Maryland School of Medicine in a study published in 2001 by Linda Chavez titled "Judging a Doctor by His Skin Color." She reported that affirmative action students graduated at a rate of 68% while Whites and Asians did so at 82%. Furthermore, 25% of these affirmative action students failed to pass the U.S. Medical Licensing Examination. This higher dropout pattern among affirmative action students continues to be observed. Unfortunately, many such individuals are left without a degree and with a debilitating debt burden. Even those who perform well and manage to graduate are often considered a product of a policy and not well-earned merit.

Many people feel it is not acceptable to lower academic standards, especially if the U.S. is to remain at the forefront of science, technology, and innovation (STEM), just to meet race-based admissions quotas. Such minority graduates, who did have merit and performed highly, are potentially discriminated against, and stigmatized by future employers who may see them as insufficiently educated and of low ability. In this system of race-based admissions, it has become clear, most are not benefited. The pendulum has swung in the direction that merit should be the only standard for new applicant admissions. Latinos as a community agree with this concept. They do not want a free ride or race-based handouts. Latinos are more than talented enough to succeed without such race-based maneuvers that discriminate against others. The California experience with affirmative action policy is indicative of this phenomenon. In 2020, California voters rejected Proposition Sixteen with 56.1% of the votes against it. There were 6.4 million votes

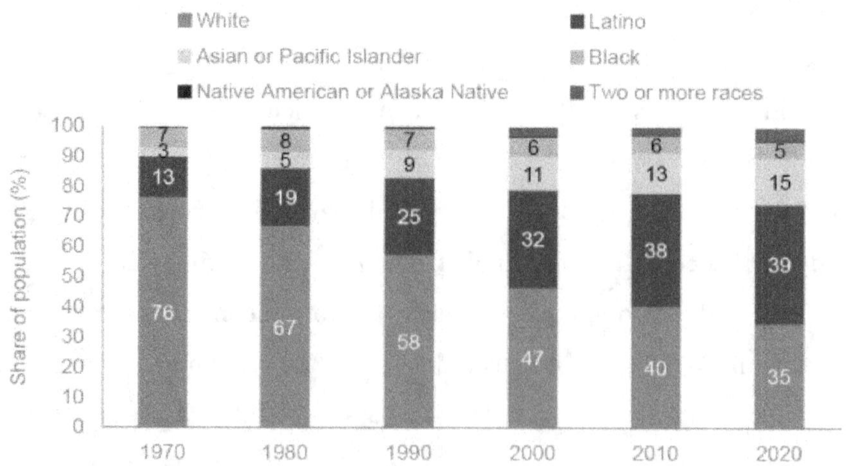

against and 5 million for it. This proposition was designed to overturn Prop. 209 which banned affirmative action in 1996. Considering that in 2020 the California population was made of 35% White, 39% Latino, 15% Asian, 5% Black, and 4% Multiracial (see graph), merit-based college admissions serve to demonstrate an interesting pattern. For example, the incoming first-year class of 2015 at multiple California institutions such as U.C.L.A., U.C. Santa Barbara and U.C. Berkely, clearly demonstrate the overrepresentation of Asians and the significant increase in Latino enrollment without affirmative action. Whites and Blacks were represented at close to their population percentage (see charts). Here are the actual percentages: U.C.L.A. had 35% Asian, 31% White, 24% Latino, 6% Multiracial and 4% Black. At U.C. Santa Barbara they were 34% White, 31% Latino, 22% Asian, 10% Multiracial and 4% Blacks. At U.C. Berkely they were 46% Asian, 30% White, 15% Latino, 6% Multiracial and 2% Black. At U.C. Irvine there were 41% Asian, 36% Latino, 15% White, 4% Multiracial and 3% Black. Interestingly, according to the California Department of Education, the 4-year graduation rates in 2020-21 among the various racial groups were 94.1% for Asians, 88.2% for Whites, 80.5% for Latinos and 72.5% for Blacks. The 5-year graduation rates for 2020-21 were higher with 95.0% for Asians, 90.3% for Whites, 85.4% for Latinos and 80.7% for Blacks (see table). These percentages are significantly higher than the 5-year national average graduation rate for every racial group, which according to educationdata.com (February 2021) were: 69.3% for Asians, 62.2% for Whites, 41.5% for Latinos and 40.5% for Blacks. What about the highly prestigious Ivy League institutions still implementing affirmative action policies?

As an example, the incoming 2015 first-year class at M.I.T. was 40% White, 30% Asian, 16% Latino, 8% Multiracial, and 6% Black. Johns Hopkins University had the exact same percentages for Whites, Asians, and

Latinos, with the difference that 8% were Black and 5% Multiracial. Harvard University had 47% White, 24% Asian, 13% Hispanic, 8% Black, and 7% Multiracial. Princeton University, Cornell University, University of Pennsylvania, Yale University, Columbia University, and Brown University all had remarkably similar percentages as Harvard (see charts). It is evident Latinos and Blacks at these highly sought after institutions remain underrepresented despite affirmative action policies. Also, as stated previously, observed graduation rates are much lower among affirmative action students than those admitted in California, a non-affirmative action state.

4– Year graduation rates by ethnicity

Student Group	2019–20 4-Year Graduation Rate	2020–21 4-Year Graduation Rate
African American	76.8%	72.5%
American Indian or Alaska Native	75.8%	73.0%
Asian	92.5%	94.1%
Hispanic or Latino	82.1%	80.5%
White	87.8%	88.2%
Two or More Races	85.5%	85.5%

www.cde.ca.gov

5– Year graduation rates by ethnicity

Student Group	2019–20 4-Year Graduation Rate	2020–21 4-Year Graduation Rate
African American	80.4%	80.7%
American Indian or Alaska Native	78.7%	79.8
Asian	95%	95.1
Hispanic or Latino	85.1%	85.4%
White	90.2%	90.3%
Two or More Races	87.9%	88.8%

www.cde.ca.gov

If one closely examines these numbers, it is evident Asian students are also overrepresented at Ivy League Universities, but Whites are not anymore. According to the U.S. 2020 Census, Asians are 5.9% of the U.S. population, Whites 57.8%, Latinos 18.7%, Blacks 12.1%, Multiracial 4.1%, and others 1.4%. By a significant margin, Asians are the best students in the U.S. and haver the highest graduation rates. Should universities in the U.S. punish these individuals and many Whites for their high merit beyond SAT scores? Or, instead, allow the California merit-based model to become the rule? There is no doubt that if K-12 grade academic deficiencies become the priority of a national program, not only targeting minorities in need, but also disadvantaged Whites, soon enough the percentages of incoming first-year students at IVY League Universities will parallel the U.S. population, with Latino and Black minorities achieving admission of their own accord and merit. This is not a matter of innate intelligence or ability, but of providing the necessary resources early in the educational process, critically vital for future success.

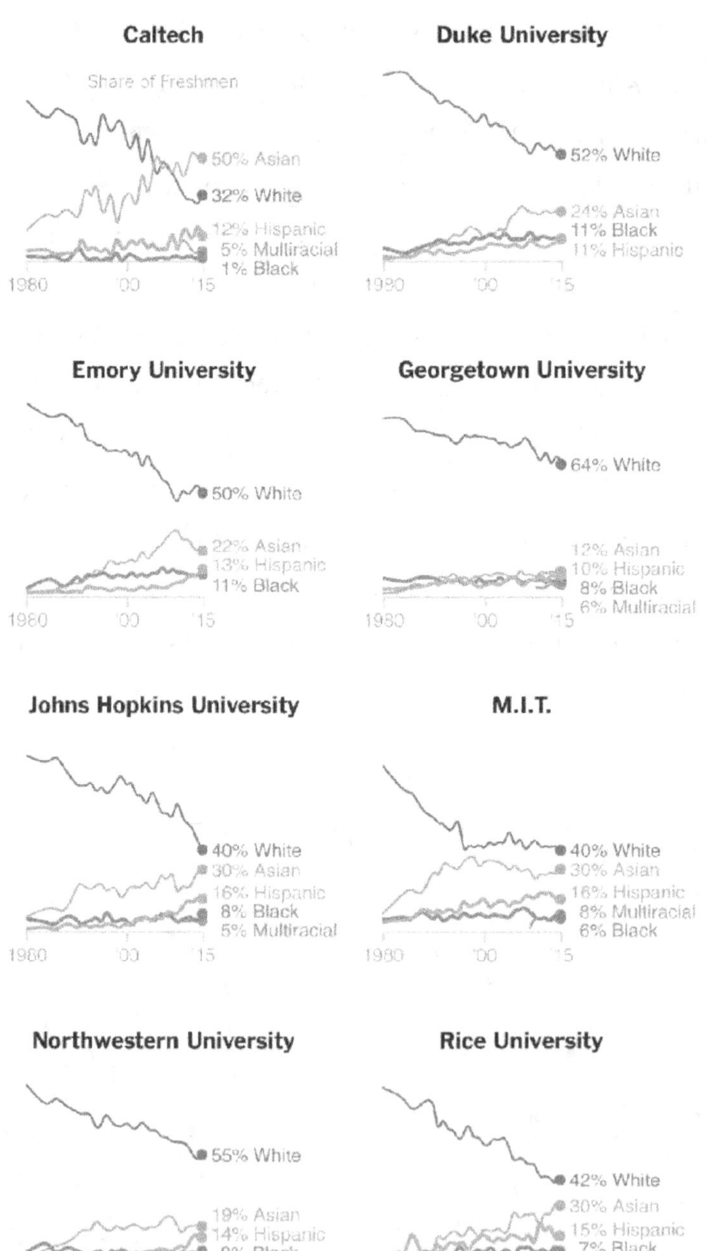
Caltech
Share of Freshmen
50% Asian
32% White
12% Hispanic
5% Multiracial
1% Black
1980
'00
'15

Duke University
52% White
24% Asian
11% Black
11% Hispanic
1980
'00
'15

Emory University
50% White
22% Asian
13% Hispanic
11% Black
1980
'00
'15

Georgetown University
64% White
12% Asian
10% Hispanic
8% Black
6% Multiracial
1980
'00
'15

Johns Hopkins University
40% White
30% Asian
16% Hispanic
8% Black
5% Multiracial
1980
'00
'15

M.I.T.
40% White
30% Asian
16% Hispanic
8% Multiracial
6% Black
1980
'00
'15

Northwestern University
55% White
19% Asian
14% Hispanic
8% Black
4% Multiracial
1980
'00
'15

Rice University
42% White
30% Asian
15% Hispanic
7% Black
5% Multiracial
1980
'00
'15

U.C. Berkeley

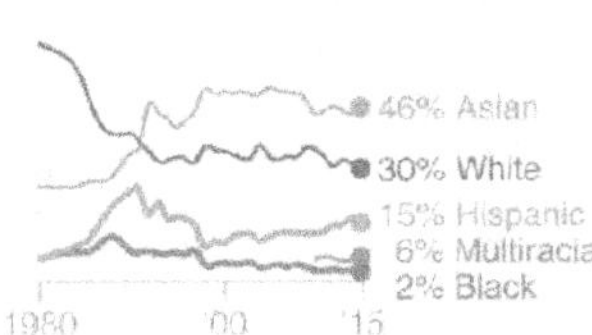

U.C. Davis

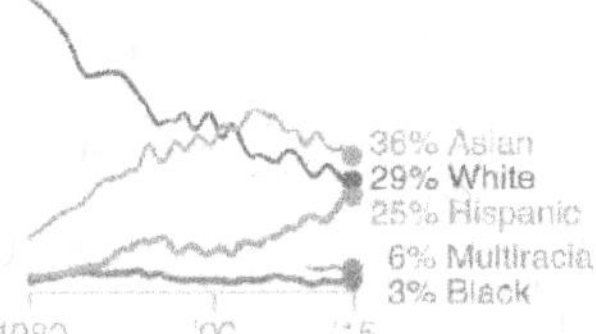

U.C. Irvine

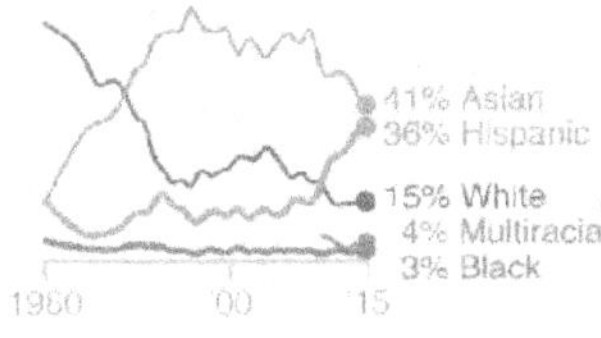

U.C.L.A.

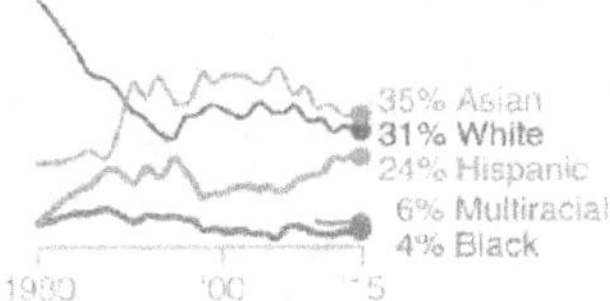

U.C. Merced

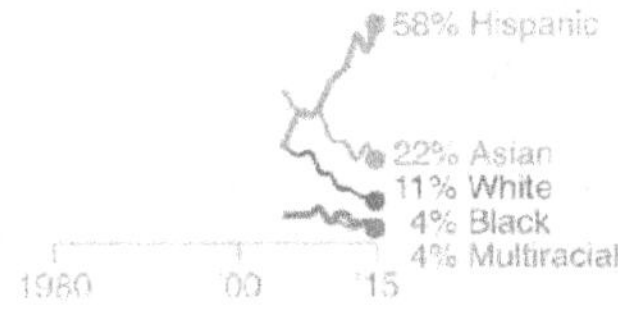

U.C. Riverside

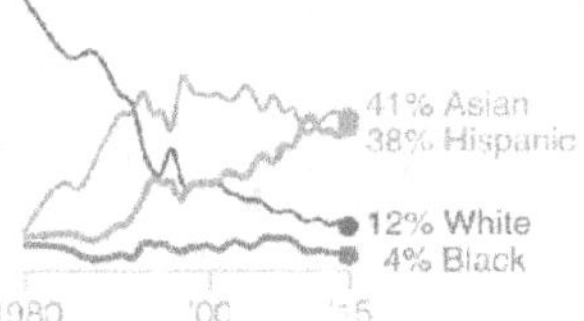

U.C. San Diego

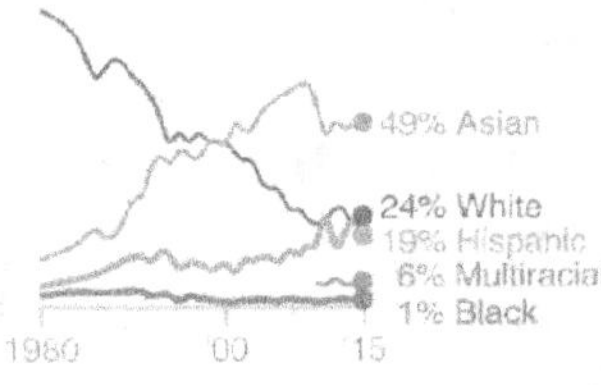

U.C. Santa Barbara

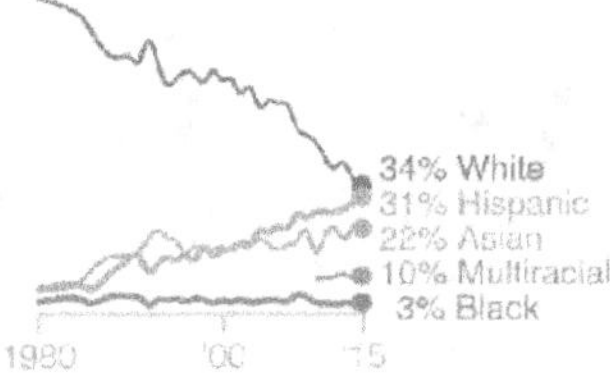

Brown University

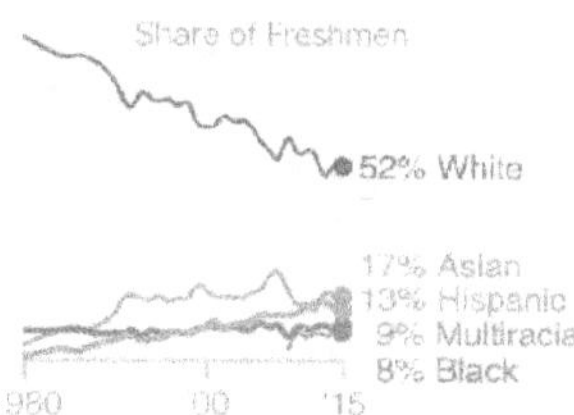

Columbia University

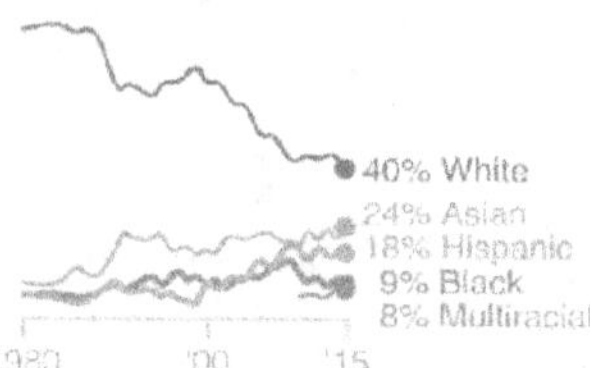

Cornell University

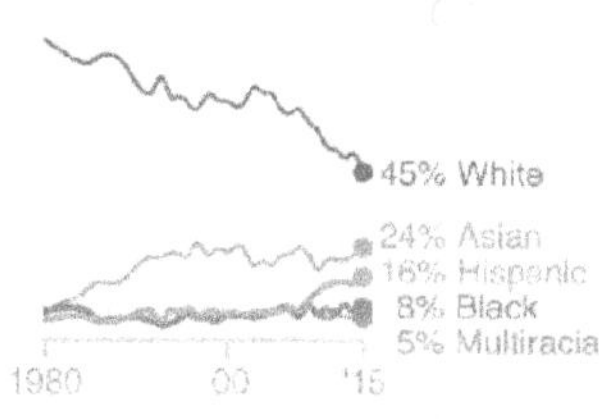

Dartmouth College

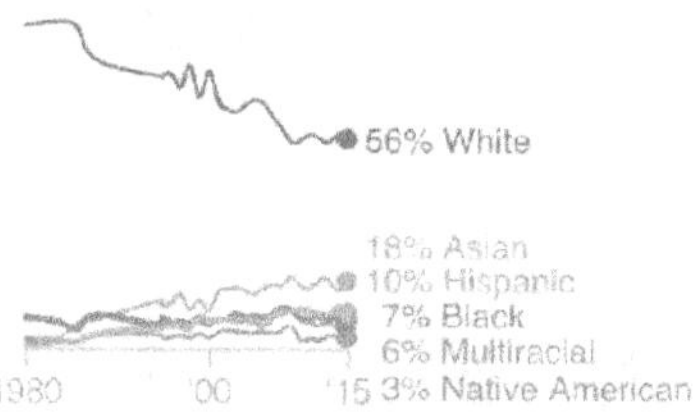

Harvard University

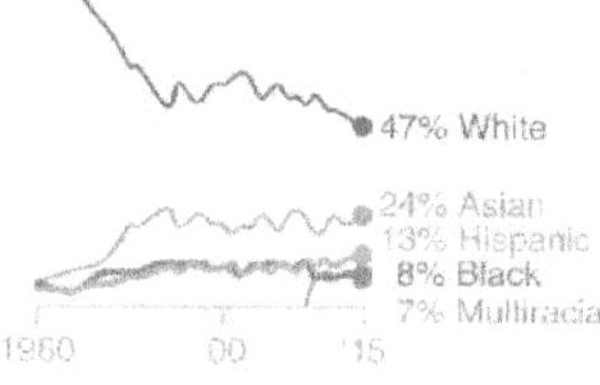

Princeton University

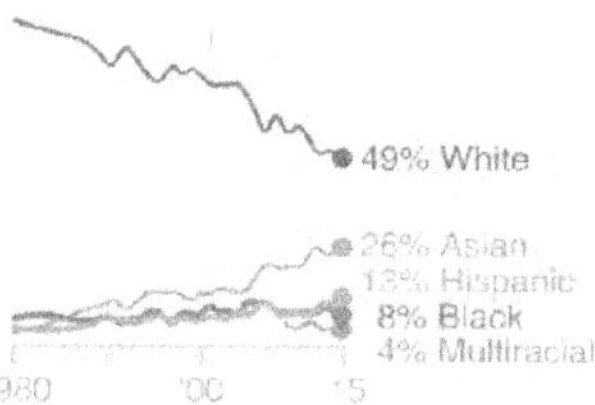

University of Pennsylvania

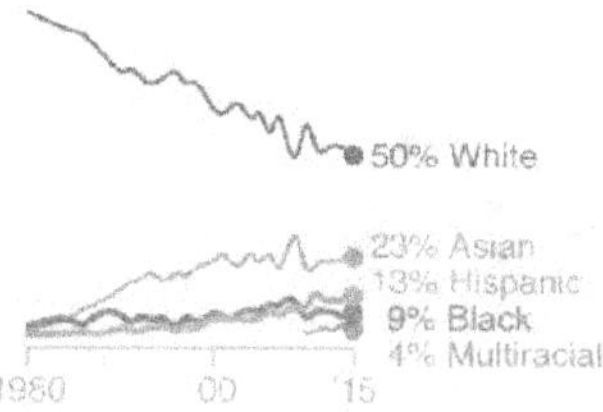

Yale University

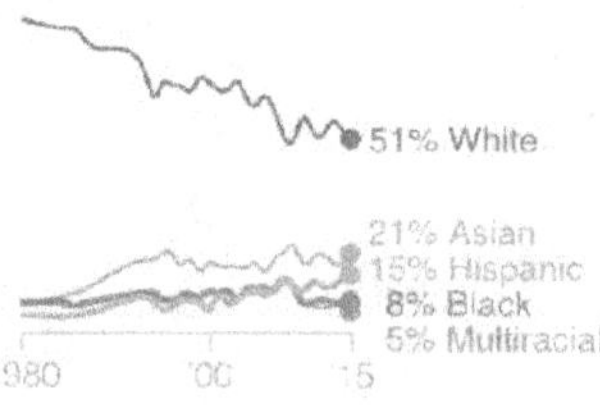

We now have come to understand that band-aid policies do not make up for past injustices. Affirmative action does not eradicate discrimination as was originally intended. Simplistic diversity of race quotas, as noted above, does not result in higher academic performance or higher graduation rates. For example, would anyone feel greater confidence and trust in a medical doctor or surgeon who had underperformed academically in high school, in pre-med, and even in medical school, at times unable to pass licensing exams? How about a lawyer or a judge? Or a structural engineer or an architect? Or a pilot? How about military leaders? I believe most of us want top professionals to provide care and expertise or other valuable services to every community and to the country at large. Race, ethnicity, skin color, gender or sexual orientation should not impact the college admissions criteria nor the many professionals that we will all encounter in life.

In fact, the real problems occur much before high school, mostly in elementary and middle school public systems. Unfortunately, the Covid-19 pandemic, on account of government-imposed public school lockdowns, has had catastrophic consequences in academic performance. There has been an almost two-grade delay in math, reading, and writing skill advancement, along with social and community development. This now presents a tremendous catch-up challenge for most public school districts in order to avoid even larger numbers of poorly prepared students for college in the coming years. This is indeed a national emergency. Lawmakers, parents, and other stakeholders urgently need a call to action to resolve the deficits in these lower socioeconomic communities' K-12 schools, to gradually raise academic standards and parental involvement in their children's education at all levels, instead of the opposite. Individual and collective excellence will not come by accident or by well-wishing or by lowering admission standards for higher education or by race-preferred status. No matter the pending decision at the U.S. Supreme Court on affirmative action, it is time to understand why, from both an academic and household income standpoint, Asians are the most successful individuals in the U.S. No doubt, we can all learn and follow their example of excellence!

MIDDLE CLASS STATUS

The increasing numbers of Latinos considered middle class is likely to result in even more high school graduates applying for college and university admissions, as noted above by the dramatic increase in the number of applicants over the last twenty years. We have already noted that if the Latinos in the U.S. were an independent country, their collective GDP would be the fifth largest in the world. Back in 2015 they were the seventh largest. According to a U.C.L.A.'s Center for the Study of Latino Health and Culture study, between 2010 and 2015 Latino GDP grew at a 2.9% rate annually, outpacing overall U.S. growth of 1.7%. In the coming decades the economic strength and productivity of Latinos, especially with median age of twenty-eight years, and more gravitating to science and high-tech fields, Latinos will continue to outpace all other groups in the U.S., in parallel with their impressive population growth. Is it Latinos will overtake

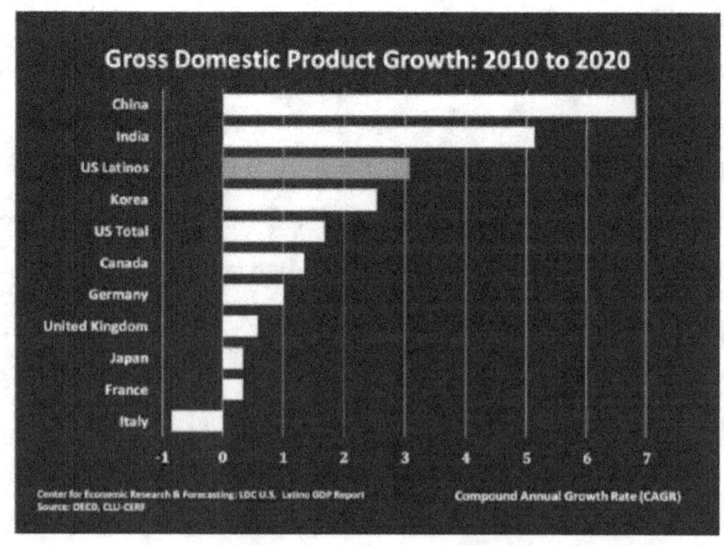

Germany and Japan over the next ten to twenty years in world GDP ranking, behind China and the U.S.? As this is occurring the Latino middle class has been growing. As of 2021, 49% of Latino adults are considered middle class in the U.S. According to the U.S. Census Bureau and the Beacon Economics Report, the median income for Latinos continues to rise with more becoming affluent as poverty rates decline. Latino business ownership has increased exponentially over the last ten years. All this economic prosperity is a consequence of higher high school graduation rates, more college enrollment, and a narrowing Latino education gap. In the last ten years, the Latino highly skilled workforce has increased by 36% overall, with a 52% growth in computers, 28% in healthcare, and 27% in business management and science. By 2025, Latinas are expected to grow from 18% to 25% of the nursing population. Many more indicators of Latino surging consumer power in different areas of the U.S. economy are evident. Different examples include the fact that Latinos represent some 46% of new home growth, 68% of auto industry growth, and by 2050 some 53 million will be NFL fans, up from 30 million in 2020. It would not be surprising if in time, by 2050, Latinos will be at least equal to Whites, by percent of their respective population, as the most numerous in the all-important U.S. middle class! For most, this represents the attainment of the American Dream, with complete assimilation, adaptation, acceptance, and love of the U.S. as a country and its culture, while many will undoubtedly still maintain deep-rooted attachments to their ancestors' nation of origin. Latinos, are a content group, enjoying greater prosperity than at any time in U.S. history and in comparison, to many of their relatives and friends still back in their country of origin.

LATINOS AND ENTERTAINMENT, MEDIA, AND ENTREPRENEURSHIP

Latinos are shaping the national and global culture. Latinos have become a growing and powerful force in most aspects of American society. Latinos have become a savvy and avid media consumer group, especially the highly sought-after 18–34-year-old demographic, of which they are now more than twenty percent and will grow up to twenty-five percent in the next five years. Aside from media consumption, Latinos are making significant contributions in the radio, film, and movie industries. They are also sensitive to their image, now more than ever calling out programing with anti-Latino sentiment and content, and at the same time rewarding with higher ratings and revenue programs and movies that feature Latino talent, enhance cultural and family values, provide interesting storylines, and dispel negative stereotypes. Increasingly, Latinos are making contributions as digital communicators, on-line content creators, and to traditional radio, television, and film industries.

The digital revolution has been embraced by Latinos with some 78% as active smart phone users, as opposed to 68% of the general U.S. population, 11.1% Twitter use versus 6.7% of non-Latinos, and 17% more likely to access the web via their phones or computers. In fact, Latinos on average spend six hours a day on social media, 40% spend more than five hours a week listening to online music, and 34% of Latinos are eSports fans versus 18% of non-Latinos.

It can be said that Latinos are critical to corporate America. According to the 2019 LDC U.S. Latino GDP Report, Latinos as a group represented the largest purchasing power of all minorities with approximately $1.9 trillion (about $5,800 per person in the US). In the same 2019, Black purchasing power was $1.6 trillion (about $4,900 per person in the US), Asians $1.3 trillion (about $4,000 per person in the US), and Native Americans $140 billion (about $430 per person in the US). For 2023, The Selig Center for Economic Growth predicts Latino purchasing power will reach $1.92 trillion (about $5,900 per person in the US), Blacks $1.53 trillion (about $4,700 per person in the US), Asians $1.33 trillion (about $4,100 per person in the US), and Multiracial $224 billion (about $690 per person.) These numbers indicate the growing importance of Latinos to the U.S. economy, which will continue to expand in the coming decade.

If all of this is true, combined with the upward Latino mobility to middle class noted above, why are Latinos still not valued and remain underrepresented in key English language mainstream media, television, film industry, and corporate America, including Fortune 500 companies? Are movie and film executives not aware that in 2020 Latinos accounted for 29% of all movie ticket purchases? Do they not know in 2021 Latinos had the highest per capita attendance, going to the movies an average of 1.7 times that year, compared to 1.3 times for Blacks and Whites and 1 time for Asians? Are politicians aware their ads are 1.7 times more likely to be seen by Latinos via streaming services than traditional television? The reality is that despite the significant Latino population growth and above statistics, there remains a Latino gap in the English language mainstream media and film industry.

In the report titled The Latino Media Gap, commissioned by The National Association of Latino Independent Producers and The Center for the Study of Ethnicity and Race at Columbia University, the authors outline in their executive summary what they call The Latino Media Gap. They describe the magnitude of Latino media exclusion, that despite tremendous consumer economic power and demographic growth, the relative Latino media presence has shrunk. The Latino Media Gap study examined the status of Latino participation in mainstream media and on the internet. It describes seven sections that identify critical issues to be addressed. These include rates of media participation, stereotyping, ownership, leadership, diversity policies, Latino advocacy, and Latino innovation. The findings show a modest increase in Latino media participation since the 1940s. As an example, the authors cite that the Latino population in the 1950s was 2.8%, Latinos in TV shows at that time were 3.9% of lead actor appearances and 1.5% of all lead roles, and in movie roles these were 1.3% of lead appearances and 1.7% of lead roles. By 2013, despite Latinos being 17% of the U.S. population, Latinos comprised none of the lead actors in scripted TV shows and movies. Although lead Latino men have almost disappeared from leading actor roles, a positive is the increase in Latinas and Afro-Latinos. From 2010-13, Latino men did not have any roles in the top ten television shows and movies, and fewer than 3% of supporting TV and film roles. Latinas did have 4.6% of all film appearances and 9.5% of TV supporting roles. Afro-Latino performers represented 18.2% of Latino film actors and 16.7% of TV actors, mostly in supporting roles. Behind the TV cameras the situation from 2010-13 was worse with fewer 1.1% of show creators, 2% of writers and 4.1% of directors. In movies,

Latinos were 2.3% of directors, 2.2% of producers and 6% of writers. No Latinos served as studio heads, CEOs, network presidents, or owners. Only one Latino could be found among fifty-three TV, radio, and studio executives. So much for the diversity of lip service by the various created diversity executive positions and departments. Stereotypes also continued despite efforts to change such long-standing damaging issues. From 2012-2013, 17.7% of Latino film characters and 24.2% of TV roles were tied to crime, 36.6% of TV character appearances to law enforcement, and 44.7% characters were uncredited or unnamed. This clearly promotes a limited "type casting," if not pejorative image, to Latino actors and the roles they are cast in and to Latino society at large. Since 1996, some 69% of iconic media house cleaners were Latinas. In the media, stories about Latinos constituted less than 1%, with the majority relating to criminality. As of 2013, there were no Latin anchors and only 1.8% of news producers were Latinos. This report is a bit dated since it only analyzed the status through 2013. However, the present-day situation is not much better, especially with the population and economic Latino growth. The Government Accountability Office's newest report on Latino representation on film, television, and other publishing entities, found in 2021 that Latinos make up 12% of the media workforce and 4% of industry management, demonstrating a mere 1% growth from 2010 to 2019. The media industry is responsible for informing and influencing the public about national and international political and economic topics and personalities as well as cultural issues. Clearly there continues to be neglect and at times complete omission of Latino representative voices and ideas.

Nielsen ratings evidence that Latinos are more likely to view shows and programming with Latinos in front and behind the cameras, seems to have fallen on deaf ears. Sadly, when Latinos do obtain a media job, they are often in segregated service positions with only 3% in senior management roles.

Latinas are marginally better, beating the men by only 1% in jobs as analyst/journalist and writer/author. Could anyone make a case that anti-discrimination and equal opportunity statues are not being applied to Latinos? The fact that most English mainstream network opinion shows, tilted one way or the other twenty-four hours a day, with anchors that must "dance to their corporate" political position, all too often try to manipulate Latinos to their chosen party affiliation by smearing the opposition. Latinos, more than ever, are looking for an authentic voice in English language mainstream media they can consistently trust. Latinos, who are conservative in their personal and cultural values, have become aware of the corruptness of the mainstream media, especially when they attempt to justify and impose far-left or far-right ideologies by smearing more conservative voices. The lack of Latino presence across all the media, TV, film, and digital world will need to dramatically change soon, especially as more Latinos with higher education and knowledge are able to distinguish reality from ideology, agenda-driven manipulation, fear mongering, and gaslighting. Latinos just want the news, authentic investigative journalism, and not one-sided political opinion shows masquerading as news while omitting or spinning unfavorable or poorly performing policies of their preferred party. There is at present an obvious Latino Media Gap, and, given the growing economic and political impact Latinos will increasingly exert during the twenty-first century, by necessity, it would behoove mainstream media conglomerates and the entertainment industry, including Hollywood, to grow Latino talent across the board, but based on merit and not just on physical attributes, race, or ethnicity. Are there not enough talented, meritorious Latino actors, directors, producers, writers, editors, journalists, and network anchors? Although the answer is obvious, since 2020, it is evident that the African American presence has dramatically grown across the entire media and entertainment industry, so why not

Latinos? This is not meant to be a competition between Latinos and Blacks, but rather that the mainstream media's daily predominant Black-White binary has resulted in marginalization of other racial groups, especially the largest group, except with respect to criminality or how the non-existent pan-Latino vote will sway.

The same can be said for Fortune 500 companies. About 350 of these companies do not have a single Latino on their boards and the rest only have about three percent of boardroom positions. Once again, with the growing Latino consumer power and educational accomplishments, especially many more with master's and doctorate degrees, as well as experience and merit, it would be shortsighted for these companies not to Latinize!

LATINO ENTREPRENEURSHIP

Another reason Forbes 500 companies and most other sectors of the U.S. economy should focus on Latinos as both customers and employees is the rapid growth in Latino business ownership. The April 14, 2022, Forbes publication, Small Business Strategy, reports that although U.S. small businesses are still recovering from the Covid-19 pandemic difficulties, Latino-owned businesses have significantly contributed to the U.S. economy in important ways. In the past ten years, Latino-owned businesses have grown by 44%, compared to 4% of non-Latino owned firms. The same can be said for the number of employees at Latino-owned businesses, which has increased by 55% since 2007, compared to only 8% for White-owned businesses. The 2021 State of Latino Entrepreneurship Report (SOLE) by the Latino Business Action Network (LBAN) and the Stanford Latino Entrepreneurship Initiative (SLEI), highlight the impressive economic contributions of Latino-owned businesses in the U.S. In 2018, the approximate 350,000 Latino-owned businesses generated over $460 billion (about $1,400 per person in the US) in revenue and employed 2.9 million people (about the population of Connecticut). By 2021, the estimate was that there were between 400,000-450,000 Latino-owned employer businesses. These were distributed across all sectors of the U.S. economy, more numerous in food services and some 19% in the tech industry, which is higher than the 14% among White-owned employer businesses.

According to Biz2Credit, in 2021-2022, Latino-owned firms had faster revenue growth compared to non-Latino owned businesses. In fact, Latino-owned businesses had a 4% *growth* in average annual revenue and 11% growth in average earnings, while non-Latino businesses *declined* by 4% and 11% respectively. SLEI reported an elevated level of optimism coming out of the pandemic among Latino entrepreneurs. According to the Kauffman Indicators of Early-Stage Entrepreneurship, which measures new business creation, Latinos have the highest rate of new entrepreneurs every year since 2002. From 2010 to 2013, according to the Kauffman data, the rate of new entrepreneurs fell for every ethnic group except Latinos. Since 2013 to 2021, the rate has increased for every group, with the highest increment in Latino-owned businesses. From 2013 to 2021, out of a population of 100,000 Latinos (about the seating capacity of the Los Angeles Memorial Coliseum), the number involved in running a business rose from 380 to 540. For the same time, Asians running a business per 100,000 people increased from 280 to 360, Whites from 270 to 330, and Blacks from 190 to 280. This implies that Latino-owned businesses are young, with some 48% in business for less than five years, compared to 37% of non-Latino businesses. The rapid business growth is reflected in the SLEI report which demonstrates 35% Latino-owned business growth versus 4.5% for White-owned businesses over the last decade. Gradually, access to venture capital and traditional financing sources, which were until recently not widely available to Latinos, are becoming increasingly more Latino-friendly, most importantly in the small business sector. Over the last five years, 64% of Latino-owned businesses seeking credit sought less than $100,000 in financing compared to 52%, on average, among White-owned businesses. These trends in rapid business creation and strong demand for financing are likely to persist. Over the coming decade, the prediction is that Latino entrepreneurship and sources of financing will continue to outpace all other groups in the U.S., especially with the rapidly growing number of Latinos attaining higher education and those acquiring valuable technical skill sets, including the tech sector of the U.S economy.

LATINAS

Latinas are the backbone of the Latino population in the U.S. Latinas, who may be considered a minority within a minority, know how to overcome difficulties in their personal and family lives. They are a resilient group who, no matter their burdens, remain mostly optimistic about the future and the expectation they will be better off financially than their parents. Latinas constitute a diverse group with a collective $1 trillion (about $3,100 per person in the US) a year in U.S. buying power yet are the lowest paid segment in the U.S. Young Latinas to middle-aged Latinas make anywhere from ten and up to fifty-seven cents less for every dollar a non-Latino man makes. This wage gap increases with age. For everyone hundred White men that get promoted, only seventy-one Latinas are promoted. Latinas invest more time in unpaid work than all others in the workforce. This includes double the time on household chores and three times more on caring for family members, all adding up to a little more than seven hours a day versus four hours for non-Latinas. Since 60% of working Latinas have children under eighteen, their home responsibilities are significant. Despite these real-life challenges, 80% of Latinas have significant life improvement plans and lead the creation of small businesses at almost six times faster than any other group. Latinas are the major breadwinners and decision makers in over 3 million households. Latinas are the main stabilizers of the nuclear family that frequently incorporates extended family. In fact, 50% of households are multigenerational, 44% having larger families than other racial groups. Eighty-four percent of Latinas value family time as a top priority. Unfortunately, the increase in divorce and single parent homes, as well as concomitant decreases in marriage rates, are all having deleterious effects on Latino families.

The CDC reported in 2020 the U.S. national average divorce rate was 2.3 per 1000 people. In 2021 the divorce rate in the U.S. was 45% of all marriages. The divorce demographics for adults over age 15 as reported by the CDC.gov report is noted on the table on the left. In general, divorce rates are highest in those with lower education, employed and own are homeowners. In the period 2010 to 2020, the divorce rate per 1000 people has decreased from 3.5% to 2.3%. However, women get divorced at an average higher rate of 7.7% per 1000 people, far above the national average. In terms of 1000 married residents, the CDC.gov report shows Latinas get divorced at a rate of 22%, White women at 19%, Black women at 33% and Asian woman at 11%. Once again, a lower median household income signals higher divorce rates among women, especially in states with lower median income. As noted previously, educational status also impacts divorce rates. The National Center for Health Statistics reported divorce rates per 1000 individuals of 12.5 for those with a master's degree, 14.1 for those with a bachelor's degree and 16.4 for those with high school or less educational status. A higher level of education is inversely proportional to the divorce rate. In 2021, 450 out of 1000 marriages in the U.S. ended in divorce, with 315 (70%) in those with high school or less education.

Divorce Demographics for adults over the age of 15

The CDC.gov report provides the following demographics for the divorced population over 15 years old:

- **Average age**: 45.8
- **Bachelor's degree or higher**: 30.1%
- **Employed**: 63.3%
- **Unemployed**: 36.7%
- **Living below the poverty line**: 11.9%
- **Living with children under 18**: 23.2%
- **Homeowner**: 67.4%
- **Renter**: 32.6%

divorce.com

Furthermore, marriage rates in the U.S. have also decreased over several decades. This is the case among Latinos who, according to a 2022 study by CLACLS, reported that from 1990 to 2017, an approximate decrease in marriage rates in Latinas from 56% to 46% and in Latino men from 55% to 45%. These statistics parallel the trend in the U.S. over the past thirty years with a decline from 60% to 50% in the general population of married men and women. In the same period, cohabitation increased from 4% to 7%, equal in Whites and Latinos. Income level also impacts marriage rates. This same CLACLS study reported that in 2017, Latinos not in poverty had higher marriage rates, 48% among men and 52% among women, than those who were in poverty (38% of men and 28% of women). According to the 2018 United States Census Bureau report on the U.S. population, among 18–34-year-old women who had an income more than $40,000 a year, only 20% were unmarried. Women making more than $40,000 a year were married (40%) or engaged or in a committed relationship (40%). In comparison, 47% with an income below $30,000 and 40% of those with an income between $30,000 and $40,000, cited financial difficulties as the main reason not to get married. In general, the higher income and educational brackets for all racial groups, including Latinos, are more likely to seek marriage. In addition, age at time of marriage impacts divorce rates. Data demonstrates that 48% of those who marry before age eighteen are more likely to divorce within ten years. Those who marry between ages twenty to twenty-five will divorce at a 60% rate and those who marry between ages thirty and thirty-four at a 14% rate.

What does all this spell for Latinos in the U.S.? Latinos, like other racial groups, emphasize multiple reasons to get married. These include love, desire to have a family and children, companionship, and commitment. The U.S. currently has the sixth highest divorce rate in the world with 40%-50% of all married couples filing for divorce and decreasing marriage rates from 2009 to 2019 for all racial groups, including Latinos. Therefore, the traditional Latino nuclear and extended family may be in peril. As noted previously, with the lowest marriage rates in thirty years and the second highest divorce rate in the U.S., Latinos in the next thirty years face significant challenges in terms of family dynamics. According to the 2018 National Research Center on Hispanic Children & Families report, 55% of low-income, foreign-born Latinas have entered a co-residential union (marriage or cohabitation) by age twenty, as have 58% of U.S. born Latinas. Some 30% of low-income foreign-born Latino men and 31% of U.S.-born have entered a cohabitation union by age twenty. These statistics represent definite challenges for stable

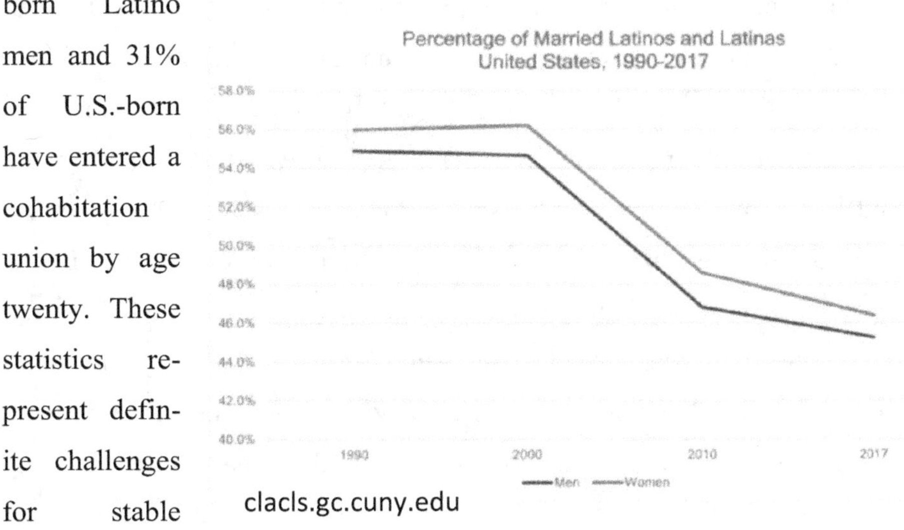

families in Latino communities.

As has been noted, early age and low-income status are both predictors of higher divorce rates and children raised in single parent households. It is imperative that a call to action is initiated in the various Latino communities to educate and inform young Latinos about the value of education, including completing high school and a bachelor's degree or higher, or conversely the acquisition of marketable skill sets, prior to considering marriage or cohabitation, and waiting to have children until such time as a more secure family-oriented status may be accomplished. All of this helps individuals avoid poverty and lowers the risk of divorce, while providing children with more well-rounded parenting, with both father and mother present, and more educational opportunities.

Per a Statista October 2022 report, the number of Latino households with a single mother in 2021 was 3,473,000. Also, in 2021, the number of single father Latino households was 1,920,000. According to the Statista Research Department report in September 2022, the total number of Latino families in the U.S. was about 14.1 million. These statistics indicate that about 38% of Latino children are being raised in a single parent household, with 63% of these by single mothers. These alarming numbers may not include all the Latinos living in the U.S., especially undocumented, long-term residents in the U.S. or millions of new migrants in the last two years. It is likely the number of Latino single parent households in the U.S. is over 40%. Given the expected Latino population expansion over the next three decades, Latino communities must prioritize to derail the above statistics. It is the Latinas and their children who bear the highest burden, resulting in higher poverty rates, lower educational attainment, lower paying employment, and more government dependence, with the risk of all these hardships becoming generational.

IMMIGRATION

The present administration's current open southern border policy, in effect since January 2021, has not been met with a favorable opinion from most of the U.S. Latino population, especially those living in the southwestern states. These most affected U.S. citizens and residents point to the adverse impact these migrants have had and continue to have on their communities. This includes an increase in drug and human trafficking, homicides, and other violent crime, over burdening of schools and healthcare systems, job competition, homelessness, and the overall disruption of the established social fabric in tight knit communities with unvetted people from diverse cultures. These migrants cross the Mexico-U.S. border illegally and then turn themselves into Border Patrol officials requesting refugee status. It is estimated most are in fact economic migrants and do not qualify for refugee status. Then, in brief time, often without background checks or vaccination status (contrary to legal visitors to the U.S., who still as of January 19, 2023, must prove they are vaccinated against Covid-19 to enter the states), they are allowed into the U.S. with a future court date. Over eighty percent of these migrants do not show up to their scheduled hearing. To deal with the massive numbers of migrants crossing our southern border daily, various state governors, to relieve the stress experienced by multiple border towns, have been bussing, and in some instances flying, individuals to so-called sanctuary northern states. This has created the anticipated political and mainstream media storm, resulting in even more divisionism in the U.S. Sadly, none of these tactics solve or provide solutions to alleviate the problems.

While many on the progressive political side desire completely open border policies, most on the conservative or right-leaning side prefer legal immigration policies and a hard-nosed approach to illegal immigration. Paradoxically, Latinos opine that the U.S. immigration system needs major

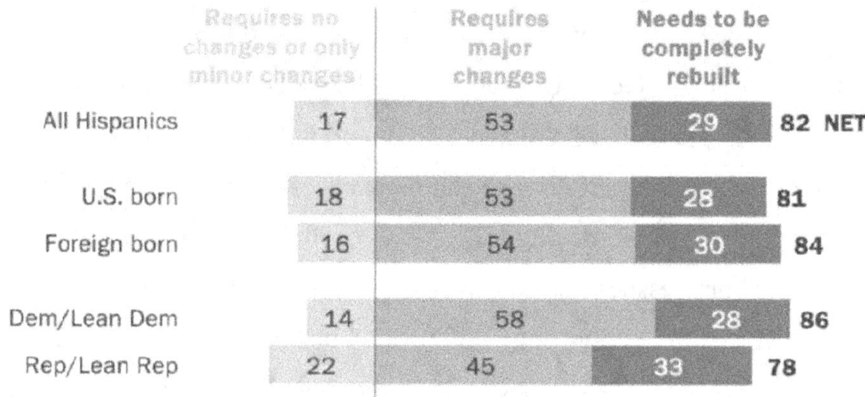

Latinos say U.S. immigration system needs major fixes

% of Latinos who say the immigration system in this country ...

Note: Based on Latino adults. Share of respondents who didn't offer an answer not shown.
Source: National Survey of Latinos conducted March 15-28, 2021.

PEW RESEARCH CENTER

fixes. According to a 2021 Pew Research Center survey of Latinos from both major political parties, 53% say major changes are needed in the entire immigration system and 29% state it needs to be completely rebuilt. About 52% of Latinos also wanted a resolution for the "Dreamers," that is those who came illegally as children, to be able to apply for legal status. Some 51% of Latinos desire to establish amnesty programs for those already illegally in the U.S. In addition, 42% of Latinos state that it is especially important, and another 33% that it is somewhat important, for the U.S. to increase security at the U.S.-Mexico border to reduce illegal crossings. Approximately 44% of Latinos and 48% of U.S. adults say illegal immigration is a very big problem today. Only about 5% of Latinos believe the U.S. has done a very good job in dealing with the influx of illegal immigrants. It is evident Latinos would get behind political leaders who could accomplish these issues: decreasing illegal immigration at the U.S.-Mexico border, with its domino effect of problems for Latino communities and the country at large, resolving the "Dreamers" or DACA stalemate, and providing a turnkey amnesty law. In addition, congress needs clarity on the per year numbers of new economic migrant applications, on how to dramatically speed up the bureaucratic process of such applications and similar issues for temporary guest worker visas, depending on labor force needs in the U.S. Fixing one or all these issues will require a thorough understanding of past immigration policies and a sharp vision of the present and future of the U.S. Only then can we determine how we got to where we are today, with more than fifty percent of people believing the immigration system is broken. To produce a universal immigration policy that addresses all the above items, let us briefly revisit the prior one hundred years of U.S. immigration policy.

THE IMMIGRATION ACT OF 1924

The Johnson-Reed Act, or Immigration Act of 1924, limited the number of immigrants to the U.S. through a nation of origins quota system. The law, signed into law by President Calvin Coolidge, was based on the 1890 national census. Immigration visas were provided to up to two percent of the total number of people from each nationality in the U.S., excluding Asians. In 1890, some 55 million out of a total U.S. population of 62.9 million (about twice the population of California) were "white," most originating from northern and western Europe, meaning that approximately 87% of the new immigrant visas would be for people originating in those European countries. In 1917, Congress enacted the first highly restrictive immigration law, upon which the 1924 law was based. The 1917 Act also implemented a literacy test, requiring immigrants sixteen years and older basic reading comprehension in any language. This restricted most Mexican immigrants since illiteracy rates were greater than eighty percent in that population. At that time, many

Mexican immigrants were subjected to humiliating delousing exposure with Zyklon gas when crossing the International Bridge between Ciudad Juarez and El Paso, Texas. In addition, the 1917 Act levied a tax on arriving new immigrants, and officials were permitted discretion on whom to exclude. Except for Japanese and Filipinos, the act excluded all those born in the "Asian Barred Zone." The Chinese were not included in the Barred Zone, but they were already denied immigration visas by the Chinese Exclusion Act from 1890. Then a republican senator from Vermont, William P. Dillingham, attempted to increase quotas by setting them at three percent of the total population of the foreign-born of each nationality in the U.S. as recorded in the 1910 census. This increased to 350,000 per year the number of available visas. In 1910, the U.S. population was 91.9 million, of which 81.7 million were White, 9.8 million Black, and 797,994 Latino. There were no quotas for those born in the Western hemisphere. President Wilson, preferring a more liberal policy, vetoed the law, believing it was too restrictive. In 1921, new President Warren Harding convened congress to reconsider the law, and it was passed in 1922. By 1924, the quota system was so widely accepted in Washington, D.C., that the discussions centered on how to adjust it. The restriction-driven advocates won the day by lowering the quota back to two percent and tracing back the origins of all people born in the U.S. including natural born citizens. The 1890 census would serve once again as the template for visa calculations. Since most people were of British and Eastern European descent, by far the largest number of new immigrant visas under the 1924 Act would be for those from Britain and Western Europe, mostly excluding all others. Those from Southern and Eastern Europe were prohibited from immigrating. No provision was made for those born in the rest of the Americas. This act also excluded all foreign-born, who by virtue of race or nationality had been ineligible for citizenship in the U.S. The existing nationality laws from 1790 and 1870 had excluded Asians from naturalizing in the U.S. The 1924 law also prevented Japanese from immigrating to the U.S. The clear message from the restrictive Johnson-Reed Act of 1924 was the preservation of U.S. Anglo-Saxon homogenous culture and hegemony. In 1927, a new quota took effect based on each nationality's share of the U.S. census population of 1920. This quota system remained in place until 1965.

The Immigration and Nationality Act of 1952 (The McCarran-Walter Act) upheld the 1924 national origins quota law, except that it ended the Asian exclusion. It also introduced a system of preferences based on skill and family reunification. The Cold War influenced these lawmakers by limiting potential immigrants from countries with communist ties and continued to favor Northern and Western Europeans. This new act revised the 1924 law by allowing national quotas at a rate of one-sixth of one percent of each nationality's population in the U.S. It based its calculation on the 1920 census, with the result being that eighty-five percent of all available new immigrant visas (154,277/year) were awarded to Northern and Western Europeans. Once again, immigrant quotas for those born in the Western Hemisphere were not included and the Act continued to discriminate against Asians, resulting in limited Asian immigration.

The Immigration and Nationalization act of 1965, known as the Hart-Celler Act, and now as the 1965 Immigration Act, abolished the national origins law, the standard since the 1920s as previously noted. This in fact ended the immigration preference for Northern and Western European peoples, ending the long-existing discrimination against all others. The bill received wide support from northern Democrats and Republicans, but mostly opposed by Southern Democrats. In total, 85% of Republicans and 74% of Democrats in the House of Representatives and Senate, voted to pass the bill. Most of the no votes were from Southern Democrats. The Act created a seven-category preference system that gave priority to relatives and children of U.S. citizens and legal permanent residents, professionals and others with special skills, and refugees. It did however maintain a per-country and total immigration limits. For the first time it set numerical limits on immigrants from the Western Hemisphere (Latin Americans and Mexico), capped at 120,000 annually. In 1969 a total of 157,306 new immigrant visas were awarded with 62.6 % to Europeans, 33.7 % to Asians, and 2.92 % to Africans. In 1970 there were a total of 172,546 new visas given, with 57.3% to Europeans, 37.8% to Asians, and 3.9% to Africans. Clearly from these visa numbers, in the immediate aftermath of the passage of the law, new visas to Latinos were negligible. Proponents of the act, including senator Edward Kennedy, argued that it would not have a significant effect on immigration or change U.S. society or culture in any significant fashion. They could not have been more wrong!

The elimination of the national origins formula and the numbers restriction on immigration from the Western Hemisphere resulted in rising numbers of undocumented immigrants encouraged by the need for workers by U.S. employers, arriving mostly from Mexico to the southwestern states. This led to the various policies in the Immigration Reform and Control Act of 1986 (IRCA), also known as the Simpson-Mazzoli Act or the Reagan Amnesty, designed to significantly reduce illegal immigration across the U.S.-Mexico border that had resulted in many undocumented workers to permanently settle in the U.S. This became a central tenet of anti-immigrant activism and rhetoric of the 1980s, apprehension and deportation of undocumented individuals, greater militarization at the border and focus by the media on the criminality of undocumented immigrants. These sentiments targeted mostly Mexicans and resulted in further anti-Mexican sentiment The practical terms the IRCA had four main policies. It reset the Registry Act of

1929, which had been previously changed in 1948, and in 1972. This meant that undocumented immigrants who has been continuously living in the U.S. prior to 1972 could apply for permanent residence. This allowed some 60,000 people to acquire legal status in the U.S. The 1972 registry date remains in effect today. The second component allowed those undocumented individuals who had been living in the U.S. prior to 1982 and could extensively prove such status, as well as farm workers who had been employed for at least ninety days in the year prior to the law's passage, to apply for legal residence in the U.S. Some three million applied within the one-year stipulated timeframe (May 1987 to May 1988). Two point seven million were approved with three-quarters from Latin countries, the majority from Mexico. The third component was that U.S. employers could not knowingly hire undocumented individuals. If they did so, they would face warnings, strict fines, and criminal proceedings. The fourth policy increased border security, with higher budgets for the Department of Labor and Border Patrol, mainly at the established ports of entry. The goal was to halt unlawful crossings and illegal workers. Many rural portions of the border, however, were left mostly unprotected.

What were the results of the IRCA? Although IRCA did not encourage illegal immigration, it failed to curb it. In the immediate years from 1986-1988, illegal immigration decreased slightly, but then returned to pre-IRCA levels. The number of undocumented individuals in 1986 were about five million. By 2013 the number was estimated to be about eleven million. In 2022, a conservative estimate is that there are between twenty to thirty million undocumented people living in the U.S. No one really knows. In the late 1980s and 1990s, many U.S. employers got around the IRCA stipulation about hiring illegals from middle-men contractors who took a portion of the employees' wages. Employers at times used discriminatory lower salary tactics to anyone who "looked" foreign to compensate for fines in case some workers were proven to be undocumented. A study by Joshua Linder titled *The Amnesty Effect: Evidence from the 1986 Immigration Reform and Control Act* found that "economic conditions in Mexico have the greatest impact on the flow of undocumented immigrants." In 1994, at the end of the Carlos Salinas presidency, Mexico sustained a catastrophic economic crisis, with several currency devaluations, extreme unemployment, and the Zapatista Movement in southern Mexico, all contributing to the flow of economic migrants into the U.S. Also, the enforcement by Border Patrol at predictable junctions opened the way for more rural crossings and encouraged new tactics such as "coyotes" and tunnels. In addition, the Mexican drug cartels had become far better organized during the late 1980s and throughout the 1990s and 2000s. A 2014 study in the American Economic Journal: Economic Policy, found that the IRCA caused an increase in crime, especially felony drug charges and apprehensions by restricting employment opportunities for unauthorized migrants, especially for those from Mexico. In retrospect, it has become evident the IRCA was only partially successful in its intent, and while unintentional, created a domino effect of consequences that resulted in more undocumented immigrants, mainstream media vilification of Latinos, and dramatic increases in drug and human trafficking into the U.S.

Fast forward to 2023. With over five million undocumented migrants crossing the southern border over the last two years, mostly unvetted, without knowledge about their covid-19 vaccination status, plus at least 600,000 or more got-aways just in 2022, and most of them released into the U.S., clearly this way of handling immigration is not a viable solution to the partly broken system. The present failure by the federal government to control the flow of undocumented immigrants has already caused multiple societal problems for the U.S. at large, mostly for minorities in whose communities they will settle, but especially for many Latino communities at and beyond the southern border.

Today, we fully recognize the framers of the U.S. Constitution went too far in the 1790 Naturalization Act by excluding all non-white people from eligibility to naturalize, allowing only "free white persons of good moral character" to become citizens. Sadly, it was only after the passage of the Thirteenth Amendment to the Constitution in 1865, that five years later in 1870, the right of citizenship was finally extended to those of African origin. The exclusionary immigration laws of 1917 and 1924, with a focus on national origin quotas predominantly favoring Northern and Western Europeans, and the 1952 law, that despite removing Asian exclusion and promoting family reunification and skills-based policies, basically continued with the status quo from 1924. By today's moral and ethical standards, these immigration laws were still exclusionary and racially motivated. The 1965 immigration law finally removed the national origins quotas, and this resulted in a flow of many more immigrants from Asia and Africa, although most continued to come from Europe. The 1986 immigration amnesty law, as we have seen, helped some but it also created downstream issues that have yet to be resolved, including the fact that we now have more than twenty million undocumented immigrants residing in the U.S., although no one really knows the actual number. With millions more currently pouring in, the situation has reached a critical level and an immediate solution is clearly needed. In addition, we still have the unresolved 2014 issue passed By President Obama, of DACA (Deferred Action for Childhood Arrivals) and DAPA (Deferred Action for Parents of Americans and Lawful Permanent Residents). These are on hold due to the fact twenty-six states presented a legal challenge to these policies. The simple question is where do we go from here? We as a country cannot continue to ignore the fact the system needs immediate fixing and should no longer just kick the can down the road. Are current office holders in congress prepared to put aside political partisanship to get these serious matters resolved? What follows are potential solutions.

IMMEDIATE CONTROL OF THE BORDER

In order to have bipartisan support in the house and senate, it is imperative that the current border crisis is brought under control. The almost 2.4 million unlawful crossings in the last fiscal year (October 2021-September 2022) represent an alarming, out-of-control situation. Immediately, human and technological resources must be brought to the border to enforce the law. Unless this is achieved in the next six to twelve months, it is unlikely significant federal immigration reform can be accomplished. The current administration's failure over the last two years to contain the flow of more than five million migrants simply walking across the southern border will need to be dealt with by the post-mid-term election congress. This is not a matter of racism, prejudice, or of a lack of humanitarian and compassionate policies. (I am Latino, a first-generation immigrant from Mexico.) Instead, it is an absolute need to protect the sovereign border of a nation for the benefit of all residents and citizens, or the nation will gradually lose its identity and security. It is interesting the billions of dollars the U.S. spends on helping other countries secure and protect their borders but does not do the same with its own.

I dream of a dialogue and negotiation at the federal level on the optimal approach to address each component of immigration law. If we have serious representatives who are interested in what is best for our country and its citizens, this will happen. This is an extremely complex topic that over the last several centuries, as noted in the previous brief review, has gradually shifted from a national origin, European-centric predominant pattern to a new paradigm that allows people from all continents to come to the U.S. The intent was to permit about one million legal immigrants, applying via lawful channels, into the U.S. per year. At the same time, per the IRCA of 1986, the amnesty program as well as internal and strict border enforcement was supposed to curb illegal immigration, yet the opposite happened. Lessons have been learned. There are almost equal numbers of politicians, immigration experts, informed media personalities, and academicians who stand on opposite sides of the question of what to do next. The first step is to control the current border crisis with strict border enforcement resources and protocols that do not simply release migrants into the country along with a publicity campaign announcing the U.S. will shortly institute new immigration policies. In the meantime, only legal applications will be considered unless an individual has genuine refugee status and seeks asylum. These may be fast-tracked. The following narrative describes potential programs for distinct groups of immigrants.

ECONOMIC IMMIGRANTS: A PATHWAY TO CITIZENSHIP

It has become evident that most current arrivals at the U.S.-Mexico border are economic migrants and not refugees. This represents a significant difference. These are individuals and families seeking a better life in the U.S. since they lack opportunities in their home country. They come voluntarily. They are not being persecuted politically or religiously. They have not been victimized by a natural disaster. What is needed is a technology-based application system from their nation of origin that is affordable and able to expedite the process to less than thirty days. An individual may apply on-line, providing all necessary information to allow INS agents in the U.S. to review all pertinent documents and perform a background check. A minimal fee such as $100-$300 could be charged for this initial application process. Ideally within thirty days while the applicant waits in their country, an answer would be electronically sent to the individual and family members who were part of the application process. If a visa is awarded, the individual travels to a designated port of entry, which could be an international airport or at the border where an INS agent would provide the visa and work permit with instructions on a hearing in one to two years to obtain green card status in three years and eventual residency pathway three years after that. The entire process takes seven years. The individual would be subjected to protection and responsibilities under the U.S. Constitution, including paying taxes, access to medical services, education for dependent children, a visa for the spouse that was included on the initial application, and the freedom to legally visit family in their country of origin. In addition, the individual and family members must remain felony free to avoid deportation and to maintain the pathway to citizenship. Children born in the U.S. to such legal immigrants are protected citizens as all others born in the U.S. Those who are denied entry on their original application may apply a year later or as indicated by INS.

It may be necessary to advertise such a system on mainstream and social media outlets in different countries, so people become aware of the new system. This would hopefully have the intended consequence of avoiding dangerous trips to the border and or contracting coyotes or others, with nefarious results. Also, it is anticipated that gradually, after an initial transition period, fewer will show up or attempt illegal border crossings. It can be announced that entering illegally will result in an immediate denial of a visa and deportation. Those who have applied via legal channels will be given first-come, first-served status. A pre-appointed congressional committee may decide that in the next five years, as a realistic goal, two million legal applicants will be processed each year. This number may vary, depending on the specific labor needs of the country, the unemployment rate, the state of the economy, and other factors such as the funding status of welfare programs new immigrants are likely to need upon arrival in the U.S. Priority may be given to family reunification and to those possessing needed skills of immediate use in the U.S. labor market.

REFUGEE IMMIGRANTS

Applicants for refugee status will also use the same on-line system noted above with the exception that they will fill out the refugee status portion on the application. These individuals and their families would be given priority and will not be included in the two million per year number stated above. INS agents will review each application and decide on the authenticity of refugee status. The applicant will wait outside of the U.S. until the application is processed in fifteen days or less. If refugee status is confirmed, the applicant will be provided with an immediate visa to enter the U.S., a work visa, and a pathway to green card status and citizenship as per the above economic migrant applicants. If the applicant is denied refugee status, then the applicant has the option to apply as an economic migrant. Applicants may not apply for both economic and refugee status concurrently or the entire application will be denied.

GUEST WORKER VISAS

Thousands of immigrants are interested in seasonal work and not necessarily in a permanent residency status or a pathway to U.S. citizenship. These individuals preferring a temporary guest worker visa may do so by applying on-line directly to employment opportunities posted on an employment opportunity site, as approved by INS. Employers requiring seasonal workers across different industries may advertise the employment terms of such opportunities, outlining the type of work, location, wage, and duration. Individuals who are hired receive a temporary guest worker visa to enter the U.S. legally and proceed to the location of the work opportunity. These individuals are then registered locally by the employer at a regional or local INS office. The same taxes as any other U.S employee apply and include income, social security, Medicare, state, and other taxes. These individuals must be enrolled in an employer-sponsored healthcare insurance policy for the duration of their work visa. At the termination of the employment period, the employer will notify INS of the guest worker who completed the work term. The guest worker will return to their country of origin within a thirty-day period. If that does not occur, the guest worker will be in violation of the terms of the visa and subject to arrest and deportation. Such violators will not be able to re-apply for any type of visa to enter the U.S. for a minimum of five years. Guest workers found guilty of any felony will immediately be arrested and may be deported. These individuals will never be re-admitted to the U.S under any present or future visa program.

If the employer wishes to prolong the employment period, an employer may request on behalf of the employee, on-line or in person, an extension of the original visa prior to its expiration. Strict adherence to this protocol will be required. Employers who violate any part of the guest worker program will be fined, possibly arrested, and will lose the right to participate in present and future guest worker programs.

AMNESTY-DACA

Opponents of amnesty programs for those who unlawfully entered the U.S. point to various reasons why such initiatives result in more problems than they purport to solve. In an article published by the Federation of American Immigration Reform (FAIR) in February 2021, Pawel Styrna outlined five reasons why amnesty is a bad idea. The first is that amnesty encourages more illegal immigration. Despite good intentions, this very phenomenon occurred, as previously noted, in the years after the Reagan Amnesty of 1986. The second is that amnesty may undermine unemployed U.S. residents and citizens. The sudden increase in the supply of workers into the labor force would compete for both low and high-skilled jobs and possibly promote wage stagnation. The third reason is that amnesty will represent a short-term increase in cost to taxpayers since state and federal welfare programs might be overwhelmed. Given the likelihood that currently more than twenty million individuals would be immediately eligible for amnesty, the pressure on public schools, healthcare system, social services, housing, food availability, transportation, and others, even if temporary, would be catastrophic and inevitably result in significant tax increases to the shrinking American middle-class. In 2016 a Heritage Foundation study found that amnesty would immediately increase taxes by $1.29 trillion a year. National debt would increase as well, at least in the short-term. The fourth point is that amnesty is inherently unfair to legal immigrants. Granting amnesty to those who violated U.S. laws, by cutting in line, is unfair to those who followed the rules, respected U.S. laws, and waited patiently. Over a million people each year are granted legal permanent residency in the U.S. These individuals endure a costly, often complicated, and frustrating lengthy vetting period prior to green card approval. Many feel this legal process needs improvement prior to consideration for potential amnesty programs since those who follow the law should be prioritized and rewarded. This leads to the fifth point in that amnesty undermines the rule of law. The U.S. was founded on the principle that individuals and institutions are held accountable to and judged equally under the law. By this principle, amnesty has the potential to reward lawbreakers while holding citizens and residents accountable to obey all laws or face consequences. This could undermine trust in the laws if some perceive an imbalance, undermining trust in the legal system.

Proponents of Amnesty, on the other hand, make the case that it is a compassionate and practical thing to do. They argue that most illegal immigrants residing in the U.S. have been contributing in many ways to U.S. society, have not broken any laws, should be allowed to "come out of the shadows," and should be given an opportunity to fully integrate into society at large. Most pro-amnesty activists state, from a U.S. society standpoint, that most such individuals are completely assimilated and have accepted and adapted to the predominant Anglo cultural nuances and U.S. institutions. They point to the increase in tax revenues and GDP growth that would result from legitimizing millions of such amnesty eligible people.

DACA represents one such group of minors who were brought to the U.S. prior to 2007. Most of these young individuals are completely assimilated and productive participants in U.S. society. Since the program's institution, they have been able to obtain a social security number, driver's license, and work permits, but not a path to citizenship. Individuals must apply every year and pay $500 in legal fees. Many are employed parents to more than 250,000 U.S.-born children. This single topic has just erupted into a national controversy, mostly along state and political party lines. In fact, as stated previously, there are twenty-six states currently contesting its legality. DACA came about in 2012 when the Secretary of Homeland Security issued an internal memo permitting prosecutorial discretion in enforcing immigration law. DACA was not authorized by congress. This resulted in a July 2021 ruling by District Court Judge Andrew Hanen which declared that DACA exceeded the powers delegated to the executive branch and violated the Administrative Procedure Act. Then, the Biden administration appealed to the Fifth Circuit Court of Appeals to preserve and fortify DACA. In October 2022, this latter three-judge panel agreed with the lower court that the implementation of DACA in 2012 was illegal. The court did keep DACA viable by allowing recipients to renew their status but preventing first-time applicants from applying to the program. It is likely this entire case will end up at the U.S. Supreme Court in 2023. At this moment, without congressional action prior to the end of 2022, some 600,000 individuals may be at risk of deportation, tearing apart families and preventing employment. So, political partisanship and grandstanding aside, what is the solution to this complex and highly contentious issue? Why is it necessary to have this resolved by the U.S. Supreme Court?

First and foremost, the "open border" crisis still going on in 2023 must be tackled effectively. Unless this matter is controlled, it is likely the slim Republican majority in the House and some Democrats will not agree to dialogue and debate on any amnesty program. Democrats and pro-amnesty advocates such as United We Dream, considering the opposition's position and especially since many fear that amnesty will only encourage millions more to surge the border, will need to be willing to compromise. The reality is that there is not a perfect solution. This is not about racism and such insinuations must stop. What is clear, is that Latinos in the U.S. desire better legal immigration policies and not the current open border situation. It's about fixing the obvious issues. Here's a proposal that may serve as a starting point for an effective congressional dialogue and negotiation:

- Control the U.S.-Mexico border with strict enforcement by increasing border patrol officers and supporting technology. Immediately stop the apprehend and release policies for economic migrants. A brief interview by border officials will determine who is a genuine refugee versus an economic migrant. The latter will be immediately deported back to their home nation. Such individuals will not be able to apply for at least five years for any type of visa to enter the U.S. Those meeting the refugee criteria seeking asylum will be admitted into the U.S. as per the current laws. Unaccompanied minors will no longer be admitted into the country. The current approximate 20,000 unaccounted for children already in the U.S. will need to be accounted for since the fear is that these minors are or will be victims of human trafficking. This policy cannot continue. These policies must be immediately publicized throughout the world, especially in Central and South American countries. Enforcement at the border will be critical such that the new policy message will be clear. This will hopefully have the benefit of slowing violence and drug and human trafficking at the border. A transition period, three to six months, may be instituted for such strict enforcement, allowing time to disperse the message and activate new border patrol personnel (instead of more IRS agents) and technology across the entire border and not just at the traditional entry points. It is anticipated with this strategy, given significant technological applications and advancements, there will not be a need to continue to build a wall. The following narrative also considers a program that will gradually provide legal status for millions already residing in the U.S., with the stated goal of not overwhelming multiple institutions, including INS, public education, healthcare, transportation, food security, law enforcement, childcare sectors, the economy, societal assimilation and integration, and others. State and federal budgets may be more optimally anticipated set.

    - Amnesty for the estimated twenty million or more longtime residents in the U.S. Current DACA eligible individuals who already have a social security number and work permit, will be offered a five-year path to citizenship. After an initial interview with an IRS agent, a resident green card will be provided, and the individual may apply for citizenship after two years and receive citizenship two to three years later, after a final interview with an INS agent. Conditions to successfully obtain citizenship will be felony free status, proof of student and or employment status, not an applicant of or dependent on social security and welfare programs, healthcare insurance coverage, and current with IRS income tax filings. DAPA eligible individuals (parents of U.S. citizens or legal residents), may apply to obtain a seven-year track to citizenship. At an interview with an IRS agent, applicants will provide proof of the following: greater than five-year continuous residence in the U.S., felony-free status, gainful employment, no dependence on social security and or welfare programs, and have healthcare coverage. These individuals would be provided with a work permit for two years and after that, if the above conditions continue to be met, including being current on IRS tax filings, a legal resident green card would be awarded after an IRS interview. Lastly, they may apply for U.S. citizenship in two to three years. Full citizenship would be granted in another two to three years, if all the above conditions continue to be met. DACA and DAPA applicants would be processed by INS on a "first-come, first-served basis" over a five-to-ten-year timeline. New applicants may continue to apply, including the estimated 400,000 DACA eligible individuals.

- Voting rights in local, state, and federal elections will be granted when all these individuals become legal resident green card holders.

- Others not meeting DACA or DAPA eligibility status, may apply for a path to citizenship track that will take seven to nine years. At the initial INS interview, these individuals will need to prove they have continuously resided in the U.S. for more than seven years, are felony-free, do not depend on social security and or welfare programs, are gainfully employed and or own their own business, and have healthcare coverage. These individuals will receive a work permit for the next five years and at that time, if the above conditions continue to be met, including up-to-date IRS income tax filings, they will be granted legal resident green card status. In two to three years, they may apply for U.S. citizenship and be interviewed by the IRS on a first-come, first-served basis. Those continuing to meet the above conditions will be granted citizenship in two to three years. The entire process will take nine to eleven years. Marrying a U.S. citizen during this work permit, resident green card, and citizenship application period would not accelerate the above timeline. Married couples and those not officially married but cohabitating, meeting the above criteria, would need to apply individually.

- Recent 2000 to 2022 migrants would need to meet the above criteria for application. It is estimated that some five million individuals, or more, have unlawfully crossed the border in the last two years (as of this writing). Most of the individuals apprehended by border patrol, requesting asylum and or refugee status, will need to be interviewed and vetted by INS to determine if they meet the criteria for such status. If so, they would be provided, per U.S. immigration law, immediate asylum status with all its protective statutes. If, on the other hand, INS determines an individual is an economic migrant, then their application would be placed behind those who have already applied via legal channels. They would be either deported to their home country, or in some cases, provided a seasonal work visa depending on their skill set and the labor needs in the U.S. economy. It is important not to just create an underclass of unskilled laborers who do not speak English and provide cheaper labor, and by so doing, undermine wages that may result in wage stagnation of struggling U.S. residents and citizens who live paycheck to paycheck. Continuing to allow millions of unskilled, unvetted, non-English speakers to unlawfully enter the U.S., as has been occurring, also presents other serious challenges. Apart from the wage issue, policies that overcome well-identified barriers to labor market integration are needed. Among these are training programs and certification of existing skill sets, job placement where needed, various classes on U.S. culture, history, and English language proficiency. These are bipartisan matters that must be agreed to by congressional leaders to optimally incorporate millions of individuals into the U.S. system. Most of these new migrants are not as knowledgeable about U.S. culture and society, government institutions, and the English language as most U.S. citizens and residents, hence a period of assimilation, adaptation, and integration is expected. Such programs, after an initial investment, will result in productive members of society not dependent on welfare programs, and in increasing U.S. GDP and prosperity at large. Without the organized implementation of widely available integration programs, there is a real risk that these new immigrants will not easily assimilate and just become pawns, mostly serving the elite donor classes as cheap labor underclasses. On the other hand, the idea that such immigrants will be so indebted to the political party that "let them in" in exchange for future votes, is fool's gold. Also, a country's failure to implement clearly stated, fair, humane, and compassionate immigration policies and then to consistently enforce these immigration laws, especially at its borders, undoubtedly results in the gradual erosion of a national identity and culture, while imposing an increasing economic debt burden on citizens, residents, and future generations.

LATINOS AND HEALTHCARE

The present U.S. healthcare system is by far the most expensive in the world, with National Health Care Expenditures (NHE) in 2020 of $4.1 trillion a year or about $12,531 per person. These figures, published by the CDC and National Center for Health Statistics, represent 19.7% of GDP. In addition, the Center for Medicare and Medicaid Services (CMS) Office of the Actuary released 2021-2030 projections for NHEs. With an estimated 5.1% annual growth rate, by 2027 NHE will be $5.96 trillion (about $18,000 per person in the US) and by 2030 $6.8 trillion (about $21,000 per person in the U.S.). According to the same report, by 2027 the annual cost for the 73.5 million Medicare beneficiaries will be $1.437 trillion with a per enrollee cost of $19,546. The estimated cost for the 82.5 million Medicaid enrollees will be $992 billion or $12,029 per person. Also, by 2027, the cost for those covered under private insurance plans will be $1.897 trillion or $9,384 per person. Despite these exorbitant costs, some ten percent of the current 335 million population in the U.S. remain completely uninsured. This number does not take into consideration millions of undocumented immigrants, especially those who have unlawfully entered the country in the last two years, who also do not have any kind of medical insurance coverage. It is evident, with current 2022 tax collections from all sources of about $4 trillion per year, the country will not be able to afford the present health care delivery model with its built-in wasteful spending on items and procedures that do not actually help patients. It is shortsighted to just continue funding this current model in the hopes that it fixes itself. It will not happen without a firm commitment from policymakers to put aside party politics and consider a different healthcare delivery model. The new paradigm should effectively address prevention, patient education, acute care, and chronic disease management. It must also implement effective cost containment strategies while dramatically decreasing wasteful spending, which some estimate to be about thirty percent of all NHEs. While some seventy percent of Americans support a single-payer model, such as Medicare-for-All, it is likely most people are not aware of the current NHEs or how to accomplish such a monumental task.

If we compare our NHEs to OECD nations with single-payer systems who have similar socioeconomic status, equivalent quality of medical care, and outcomes, our yearly cost difference is higher by about $6,000 per person. In 2020, the Peterson-KFF Health System Tracker analysis determined the cost per person in the U.S. was about $12,000 and the average for all other OECD countries was $5,700. Even Switzerland, with an older population, had a per person cost of $7,136. According to the 2021 CEO World Health Care Index, which ranks by country where patients receive the best medical care, the U.S stood at number 18. The top five nations were Denmark, Norway, Switzerland, Sweden, and Finland. Granted these are countries with significantly smaller, less diverse populations, and with higher tax rates, yet one can say the U.S. has not been getting its money's worth.

To add to this present situation is the growing doctor shortage in the U.S. Since the implementation of the Affordable Care Act in 2011, large numbers of primary care doctors (PCPs) and specialists have not been able to maintain viable independent offices. Some seventy percent or more of PCPs have become hospital employees and encouraged to refer to hospital employed specialists, who are frequently on procedure driven compensation packages. All these employed providers are incentivized to refer to hospitals and to perform in-hospital testing and invasive procedures. Not surprisingly, because of these provider-hospital institution relationships, medical costs have escalated, often without improving outcomes. This phenomenon has occurred across both for-profit and not-for-profit hospital institutions. As a result, rather than accept this pact, many providers decided to retire or change careers. New graduates of residency programs have not had the luxury of considering private practices due to start-up costs, low reimbursement schedules, high overhead, credentialing complexities to get on Medicare, private insurance plans, and student loan debt. Instead, most have had to become hospital institution employees. They have had to accept the above relationship. This has gradually left the U.S. with a provider shortage, estimated to reach some 100,000 or more by the end of this decade.

According to the Association of American Medical Colleges, the demand for doctors continues to grow faster than the supply, with the largest deficit in primary care. Unfortunately, to compensate for this deficit in medical doctors, mid-level Nurse Practitioners (NPs) and Physician Assistants (PAs) are now the main front-line providers, especially in outpatient clinics located in lower socioeconomic areas where most Medicaid enrollees live. Each year, many of these patients do not get to see an actual medical doctor. All too often, given lower reimbursement Medicaid schedules, such outpatient clinics overschedule patients simply to make the numbers work. Such patients do not get sufficient time with the mid-level provider to address most issues, including prevention, education on health, and control of chronic diseases. Visits are often quick and address only one or two issues. If there is a language or cultural barrier between patient and provider, the quality of each visit deteriorates. Such clinics are staffed with Medical Assistants (MAs) who work with the NPs and PAs, most of which are high schoolers who graduate from a six-month MA course. Aside from taking vital signs, drawing blood, and serving as translators, most do not possess sufficient medical knowledge. Also, most specialists, including those employed by hospital institutions, do not accept Medicaid enrollees, adversely impacting millions on Medicaid programs.

In 2021, KFF reported estimates from the American Community Survey on the distribution of the nonelderly with Medicaid by race. In the U.S. about 18.9% of the entire population was covered by Medicaid programs. The distribution of Medicaid/CHIP enrollees was 40.3% White, 18.6% Black, 29.2% Latino, 4.7% Asian/Native Hawaiian and Pacific Islander, 0.9% American Indian/Alaskan Native, and 6.3% Multiple Races. States with a higher proportion of Latinos depend even more on Medicaid programs, making up 30% to 60% of all Medicaid enrollees. These include Arizona, California, Texas, New Mexico, Nevada, Florida, New Jersey, and New York. Of those aged 0–64, 20% are uninsured, 32% are covered by Medicaid/CHIP/Medicare, and 48% have private insurance. Almost one-third of 18–24-year-old Latino individuals are uninsured. By comparison, 8% of Whites and 11% of Blacks are uninsured, 19% of Whites and 37% of Blacks are on Medicaid/CHIP/Medicare, and 75% of Whites and 52% of Blacks are covered by private insurance (See Table above). According to KFF, Latinos are the least eligible for ACA coverage among nonelderly individuals. Only 53% meet eligibility criteria for Medicaid programs (income less than 138% of the national poverty line) or tax credits for the on-line exchange insurance programs (income less than 400% of the national poverty line). By comparison, 70% of Whites and 67% of Blacks meet at least of the above criteria. Some 30% of Latinos are completely ineligible for such programs due to immigration status, while only 2% of Whites and 4% of Blacks have such issues. Furthermore, of all non-insured Latinos, 49% are not U.S. citizens, 9% are naturalized, and 42% are U.S. citizens. It is not surprising that about 20% of Latinos remain uninsured due to significantly less eligibility under the ACA and non-citizen status. What about the millions of new migrants? Will new immigrants unlawfully crossing the U.S.-Mexico border in the last two years be enrolled in Medicaid programs? Will there be enough providers and outpatient clinics to care for these individuals, especially in a language and culturally appropriate fashion? Will specialists care for these individuals? Or will many, frustrated over the difficulties in accessing care in the U.S., go

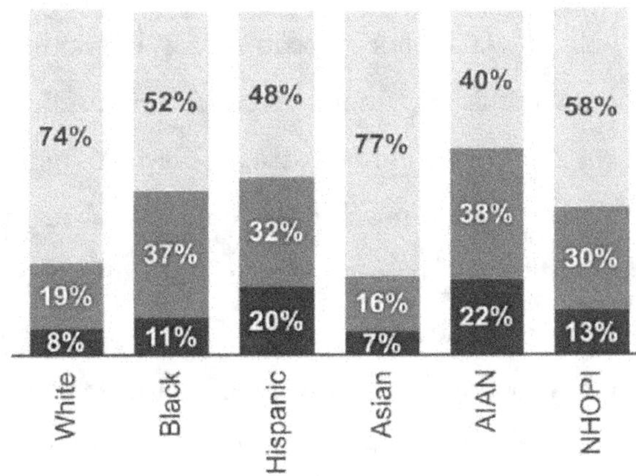

without medical care or in some cases, eventually become sick enough to warrant going to an emergency room? There are no easy answers.

All these issues are extremely important to the millions that depend on public healthcare coverage. As noted previously, the U.S. has a large public and extremely expensive healthcare delivery program. For Latinos, with some five million currently covered by Medicare and about twenty million by Medicaid, these programs are of critical importance and will continue to be a priority issue in the 2024 election. Given the expected impressive Latino population growth over the next several decades, as discussed above, it is imperative that an adequate solution is found. If one considers the increasing obesity epidemic in the U.S., with the inevitable higher prevalence of diabetes and Metabolic Syndrome widespread in different Latino populations, as also occurs in the Native American Indian populations, a healthcare crisis looms in the immediate horizon. By most estimates, some 36% to 38% of Latino adults, especially those of Mexican descent, currently suffer from Metabolic Syndrome, significantly increasing the risk of cardiovascular complications such as heart attacks, strokes, heart failure, renal failure, and the need for hospital-based services, expensive surgeries, and interventions. Latinos depending on Medicaid-driven services and the millions of uninsured individuals are not currently receiving optimal preventive health education, including nutrition, exercise counselling, effective care of acute issues, or control of chronic diseases. Most studies demonstrate that, at best, fifty percent of Latinos who have chronic diseases like diabetes, hypertension, and cholesterol abnormalities are controlled from year to year despite taking multiple medications. Lack of control of such entities eventually results in catastrophic and costly events. Increasingly, among Latino teenagers, obesity, prediabetes, and type two diabetes rates continue to grow. What will the cost in terms of morbidity, mortality, and economics be by 2040 or 2050, when the Latino diabetes and Metabolic Syndrome population will be double what we see today? Primordial and primary prevention strategies that serve to educate the U.S. population on lifestyle modification, including nutrition and exercise, must become a top priority. This needs to be accomplished by disseminating information in the public and private school systems starting in elementary schools, primary care clinics, social media networks and mainstream media programs, marketing of healthy products, health fairs, elimination of food desserts, state and federal government tax credit initiatives rewarding food industry products with reduced sugars, saturated and trans fats, and other harmful products. Promoting affordable plant-based diets, especially to minorities at risk for Metabolic Syndrome, as in those dependent on public health coverage, should be a top priority. Unless serious strategies to change the current paradigm are instituted, the horizon appears ominous. For Latinos, healthcare policy issues will play a major role in the 2024 presidential election, especially in the states with the largest proportion of Latinos. Whichever party manages to present a workable model, both financial and medical, will have the attention of Latinos and all other racial groups. Simply doubling down on the ACA, without a serious paradigm shift, will no longer suffice.

For now, I will refer the reader to my book titled, *The Blended Plan, A Medicare Optional Model* (to be published later in 2023). This is a starting point for a dialogue that will necessarily involve the public and private sectors and lawmakers at large. It is both a financial and medical model. This proposal addresses most of the issues noted above, including covering millions of uninsured individuals, allowing many to opt into Medicare or to remain on private insurance, and permitting providers to thrive independently without the current conflict of interest situation while being held accountable via quality of outcome measures. Social determinants of health are also addressed in this model, allowing medical homes to identify individual and community deficiencies from a health care perspective to effectively intervene. In addition, the Blended Plan Model proposes cost containment strategies that decrease wasteful spending and improve overall quality of care. The model lends itself to being first tested in a pilot study and improved prior to general implementation. The sooner such a model, as well as others, are considered, the better, otherwise the mounting NHEs this decade will eventually make it necessary, with drastic consequences for millions who depend on public medical coverage. Otherwise, a two-tier system, as occurs in most developing nations, with the poor, disabled, and elderly receiving inferior medical care will ensue, while the affluent access the top facilities and doctors. I do not see this as a viable option for the U.S., but it is where we are presently heading.

LATINOS AND CRIME

According to the CDC, in the U.S. the murder rate increased thirty percent from 2019 to 2020. This was the largest single-year increase since 1905, and ever. There were 7.8 homicides/100,000 people (about the seating capacity of the Los Angeles Memorial Coliseum) in 2020, up from 6.0/100,000 in 2019. In real numbers, there were 21,570 murders in 2020 and 16,669 in 2019. Most states experienced higher homicide numbers, with eight states increasing by more than 40%. Firearms were involved in 77% of homicides in 2020 and 73% in 2019. The number of cases that were closed with an arrest decreased from 61% in 2019 to 54% in 2020. The rate of aggravated assault also rose by 12% from 2019 to 2020. These statistics during the 2020 pandemic year are the result of the social unrest after the George Floyd murder in May 2020, combined with defund the police measures in multiple communities. The fact remains that the U.S. murder rate has been decreasing since the 1970s when it was 10.5/100,000 people (about the seating capacity of the Los Angeles Memorial Coliseum) and the early 1990s when it was about 10/100,000 people (about the seating capacity of the Los Angeles Memorial Coliseum). Today Americans are far more likely to die from suicide (13.5/100,000) and drug overdose (27.1/100,000) than from murder. Given the widespread 2020 to 2022 coverage by social media networks and mainstream media of multiple high-profile murders and gun violence, a July 2021 Pew Research Center survey showed 61% of Americans felt violent crime is an excessively big problem in the country today, up from 41% in June 2020. Furthermore, in a separate Pew Research Center survey, in 2021 47% of U.S. adults wanted more police funding in their communities, while only 15% wanted less funding. What about Latinos? A 2022 Axios/Ipsos Latino Poll in partnership with Telemundo, showed 44% of Latinos are as concerned about gun violence and crime as they are with supply chain issues and inflation. A pre-mid-term election 2022 poll by the Washington Post and Ipsos found that 80% of registered Latinos felt gun violence would a major issue that would influence their vote.

The El Paso 2019 murders by a white supremacist, in which twenty-three individuals were killed and another twenty-three injured at a local Walmart, brought to the forefront, if only for a moment, the fact that gun violence has a devastating effect on Latino communities and that they are at a disproportionately high risk of such violence. This horrific act of terrorism, by an indoctrinated, mentally ill young man was motivated as an attempt to prevent a Latino take-over of Texas. In 2022, the community of Uvalde, Texas, with eight-two percent Latino population, mostly of Mexican descent, sustained the murder of nineteen children and two teachers at Robb Elementary School by an eighteen-year-old deranged shooter. This tragedy received extensive national attention, including a visit by President Biden.

Despite these two highly publicized cases, gun violence in Latino communities receive little attention and is often left out of the national dialogue. In a November 2022 the Center for American Progress article by Allison Jordan, she states that from 1999 to 2020 an estimated 74,522 Latinos in the U.S. died from gun violence with violent homicides accounting for sixty percent of all gun deaths among Latinos. In fact, from 2014 to 2020, the number of Latinos who died due to gun violence increased by sixty-six percent, double the national rate. In 2020, gun violence killed 5,003 Latinos, or thirteen people a day. Ms. Jordan reported that 71% of Latinos report fear for their personal safety from mass shootings in public places and another 53% are genuinely concerned about gun violence in Latino communities. After inflation and the cost of living, polls find gun violence and crime are the next key issues for voters. Sadly, Latinos living in the U.S. are more than twice as likely than Whites to die from gun homicide. From 2019 to 2020, the gun homicide rate among Latinos rose by thirty percent, averaging 4.6 deaths/100,000 people (about the seating capacity of the Los Angeles Memorial Coliseum), compared to 2.2 deaths/100,000 people for White Americans. Assaults from 2009 to 2018 were 128.7/100,000 people against Latinos and 90.5/100,000 people against Whites. Young Latinos are preferentially targeted. Latinos twenty-four and younger are three times more likely to die from gun violence than their White counterparts. The actual numbers per year in the young are 4.4 Latino deaths/100,000 people versus 1.5 White deaths/100,000 people. In 2020, 38% of Latino homicide victims were twenty-four or younger, while 21% of White victims were in this age group. In addition, about 50% of Latino youths live less than one mile from a gun homicide that occurred in the previous year. The negative psychological impact on the mental health of young people of such nearby tragedies cannot be underestimated. About three-quarters of Latinos live in nine states in the

U.S., and not surprisingly, those with the weakest gun laws, such as Arizona, have the highest homicide rates among Latinos, three times more than their White counterparts. A Latino living in Arizona is more than four times likely to be killed by a firearm than a Latino living in New York, more than three times than a Latino living in New Jersey, and twice as likely as a Latino living in California. In Texas, the homicide death rate for Latinos is double that of Whites, and a Latino living in Texas is three times more likely than a Latino living in New York to be killed by gun violence. The numbers in Texas are greater among young Latinos with an increase in gun homicide of 37.5% from 2019 to 2020. In Florida, gun homicide rates among young Latinos from 2019 to 2020 increased by 42.3%, twice the rate of their White counterparts. Five years after the Stand Your Ground Law was passed in Florida in 2010, the homicide rate among Latinos increased by 27.9%. Interestingly, California is an outlier among states with strict gun laws. From 2015 to 2020 California had a higher gun homicide rate of 4.1 deaths per 100,000 people compared to other states with equally strict gun laws. Firearms recovered from California crime scenes are often obtained in states such as Arizona and Texas. It is clear why Latino communities want more police funding, stronger gun laws, universal background checks, a delay period prior to obtaining a weapon, prompt identification of individuals with potential mental health issues for psychiatric treatment and to prevent them from having access to firearms, widespread community education strategies to mitigate gun violence, and armed deputies at public schools. Latinos in general, are not in favor of no bail laws, of progressive district attorneys who do not prosecute or incarcerate dangerous criminals or that permit them early parole. Current data demonstrates the dangers to society when such criminals are allowed to roam free. Efforts to prevent gun violence must be coupled with strict border protection to prevent drug and human trafficking, and potential criminal elements, including terrorists, from entering the country. Many feel the open border over the last two years have and will continue to worsen gun violence in the U.S., especially in minority communities. What about police shootings?

Racial disparity in armed and unarmed police shootings remained unchanged from May 2015 to May 2020. Researchers at Yale and University of Pennsylvania, using the Washington Post database, reported in 2020 that people of color had significantly higher death rates than Whites. During the above period, there were 4740 fatal shootings. There were 2,416 Whites (51%), 1,256 Blacks (26.7%), 889 Latinos (18.8%), 93 Asians (2%), and 77 Native Americans (1.6%). Native Americans were killed at a rate ratio of about 3 times greater than Whites, Blacks 2.6 times greater, Latinos 1.3 times greater and Asians at about 0.44 the rate as Whites. Among unarmed victims, in the same period, there were a total of 735 people killed. These were 352 Whites (47.9%), 218 Blacks (29.7%), 146 Latinos (19.9%), 11 Asians (1.5%) and 8 Native Americans (1.1%). Blacks were killed at a rate 3.1 times higher than Whites and Latinos 1.45 times higher.

The latest report by Statista Research Department, published February 2, 2023, for the years 2017 to 2022, demonstrate the number of people shot and killed by the police in the U.S. For this six-year period the number of Whites killed were 2,491, Blacks 1,336, Latinos 884, Others 186 and Unknown 1,228. From 2015 to January 2023, the rate of fatal police shootings per million of the population were: White 2.3, Black 5.9, Latino 2.6 and Other 0.9. Sadly, there continues to be about 1000 people per year killed by the police, armed and unarmed. Those killed are mostly young, with an average age of thirty-four. For Blacks it is thirty, for Latinos thirty-three and for Whites thirty-eight. The above Yale and University of Pennsylvania study estimated an average of 31,960 years of life lost annually on account of police shootings in the U.S. Communities where more of these police shootings occur, aside from the individual and family suffering, report higher community rates of mental health issues. As noted previously, these difficult issues tie into the dependence on a healthcare model that is not fully capable of addressing and caring for the needs of such communities.

The solutions to all these difficult issues are not easy to find and implement. Aside from the practical use of body cameras, independent investigations, and re-training of officers and police departments found to be deficient, the fact is most solutions start at home with nuclear and extended families. Latinos are fully aware, as are most racial groups, that discipline starts at home with the presence of father and mother role models that can lead by example, gradually instilling positive individual traits such as kindness, respect, obedience, morality, adherence to a high bar of family standards, and societal ethics. It is imperative for young individuals to learn the difference between right and wrong at home. Accountability for one's actions and their consequences, instead of immediately defaulting to victimhood status and a resentful pay-back mentality, is another essential trait that is best learned at home from the presence of effective role models. Over the last twenty years it has become painfully evident, in both Latino and Black communities, the ones with higher gun violence, homicide rates, and police shootings are more likely lacking a father and nuclear family influence. Unfortunately, this pattern is also observed in White communities with similar family characteristics, especially in lower socioeconomic areas. Community, public school, and church-based campaigns aimed at reinforcing the critical importance of a father in the home and of a nuclear family as the center piece of a successful society are needed to gradually reverse the contemporary trends of steady increasing numbers of children raised in single parent households. Latino groups who maintain this simple concept as a priority will more likely raise children who acquire academic achievement or other marketable skill sets, become more entrepreneurial, ascend socioeconomically through prosperity, become less dependent on government welfare programs, and pass on such behavior patterns to the next generation. As Latinos in the twenty-first century eventually become the majority in the U.S., it is imperative that such values remain entrenched for these communities to flourish and propel the U.S. forward.

FUTURE HORIZONS

As the Latino population growth inevitably continues over the coming decades, larger numbers will be completely assimilated and adapted to U.S. culture and institutions, just like any other Americans. Principal among these is the majority born in the U.S., especially the millions attaining highly marketable and desirable skill sets, as well as higher education degrees in business and science. Foreign-born Latinos will continue to gradually incorporate into the American landscape beyond the stereotypical manual labor pool. In fact, without the rapidly growing young Latino labor force participation across most sectors of the economy, the U.S. GDP will falter. The present and future Latino contributions to the U.S. economy cannot be underestimated. Currently more Latinos than at any other time in U.S. history are participating in U.S. politics, not only as voters, but also as candidates for political office as local, state, and federal representatives. Although still lagging far behind other racial groups as a lower percent of elected officials who are Latinos, compared to the approximate twenty percent Latino U.S. population, especially at the federal level, Latinos are finally set to make a significant leap forward. This pattern has been slowly occurring with greater numbers, mostly in states with the largest Latino populations. In time more meritorious and deserving Latinos will certainly occupy key positions in government administrations. These individuals will not occupy such lofty offices on account of their skin color, genetics, gender, sexual orientation, or other characteristics that have little to do with the character and accomplishments of the person. It is this type of high performing individual, and not one selected on account of intersectional racial- or gender-based politics, who will best serve to galvanize and inspire other Latinos. This includes the younger populations from different Latino groups to reach the highest levels of private enterprise and political office to best serve their communities.

Rejecting a victim role and government dependence will remain critical for Latino communities to advance within U.S. society, since in so doing their contributions will be even more invaluable. This example will grow from generation to generation, much as it has for other highly accomplished racial groups in the U.S. The concept of the unselfish sacrifice of millions of Latinos, that well-known work ethic, especially found in first-generation individuals who arrived in the U.S. with a mission and a purpose to provide a better life for their children and extended families, remains an essential example for the younger generations of Latinos to emulate, especially those born in the U.S. The tremendous initial hardship of frequently taking on backbreaking, low-paying jobs and accepting dangerous and suboptimal work conditions, has gradually been paying off for millions of Latino families. As discussed previously, in the last decade, more Latinos than ever are graduating from institutions of higher learning, becoming entrepreneurial, rising to a middle-class status, and entering the political arena. As the twenty-first century continues, Latinos will continue to fulfill the dreams of their ancestors, whose laudable purpose has sown the fruits of their sacrifices. Most Latinos in the U.S. fully understand this long journey, and for that reason will not want to regress to dependency on welfare programs. A policy of simply adding millions of unvetted Latino migrants, to just walk across the border, to fulfill a labor shortage in the lowest salaried manual labor sectors of the U.S. economy, will no longer suffice. Such recent crass and unethical political maneuvers that have resulted in an open border with Mexico, rejected by most Latinos in the U.S. legally, will only perpetuate an underclass status to these immigrants. They will serve the elite classes from generation to generation, delaying overall Latino advancement. In fact, this will split the Latino population. There will be on one side who have fully assimilated and integrated to U.S. society, arrived legally, are long-time residents and citizens, have contributed to the U.S. in a variety of ways, and those who continue come illegally, breaking the law, and become dependent on welfare programs. This division will result in social upheaval and chaos.

As described above in the immigration section, there are distinct options to prevent such a phenomenon, including control over the U.S.-Mexico border and an efficient guest worker visa program that does not result in a pathway to citizenship. Instead, legal immigration should be driven by merit and the skill set of individuals to meet the variable year to year demands of the U.S. labor markets. Legal immigration programs should be the only pathway to legal residence and citizenship in the U.S. refugee programs should be open to those who are actual refugees and not to those pretending such status. Inevitably, in the next fifty years, the Latino population will continue to grow, thrive, and contribute to the U.S. In time, by the end of the twenty-first century, the term Latino may become an afterthought, and individuals of Latino descent will simply be referred to as Americans.